Rebels and Reformers

The aim of Zenith Books is to present the history of minority groups in the United States and their participation in the growth and development of the country. Through these histories and biographies written by established writers for young people, Zenith Books will increase awareness of and at the same time develop an understanding and appreciation for minority group heritage.

Dr. John Hope Franklin, Chairman of the History Department at the University of Chicago, has also taught at Brooklyn College, Fisk University, and Howard University. For the year 1962–63, he was William Pitt Professor of American History and Institutions at Cambridge University in England. He is the author of many books, including *From Slavery to Freedom*, *The Militant South*, *Reconstruction After the Civil War*, and *The Emancipation Proclamation*. In April 1974 Dr. Franklin was elected President of the Organization of American Historians.

Melvin I. Urofsky, consultant on this book, teaches history in the Allen Center at the State University of New York at Albany. He received his doctorate from Columbia University and has taught at Ohio State University. He is the co-editor of *The Brandeis Letters* and the author of *Big Steel and the Wilson Administration*, *Why Teachers Strike*, and *Perspectives on Urban America*.

Alberta Eiseman is the author of two previous books on the history of immigration and minority groups. *From Many Lands*, a Junior Literary Guild selection, tells the story of America's immigrants from colonial days to our time; *Mañana Is Now* deals with the major Spanish-speaking groups in the United States, their history and current experience. She has also written two novels for teen-agers, picture books, magazine articles, and reviews for the young people's page of the New York *Times Book Review*. She recently completed a series of audiocassettes featuring interviews with people who immigrated during the early years of the century. Born in Venice, Italy, Alberta Eiseman immigrated to the United States as a teen-ager and is a graduate of Cornell University.

Herb Steinberg says of himself, "I want to emphasize that I'm an artist who illustrates and not a trained illustrator." Steinberg studied for two years under Moses Soyer on weekends while in high school. He later spent three years at Tyler School of Art, Temple University. He received his Bachelor of Arts from Adelphi College and his Master of Arts from Kent State University.

He received a graduate fellowship and served as art instructor at Kent State. He has worked as set painter for a number of Broadway plays. His numerous awards include the Purchase Award, New Jersey State Museum; a Cleo for art direction; and Citation of Merit, Art Directors Annual. He has exhibited at the Pennsylvania Academy, The Butler Institute of American Art, the Brooklyn Museum, F.A.R. Gallery in New York, The National Arts Club in New York, and the Kenmore Gallery in Philadelphia.

Rebels and Reformers

Biographies of Four Jewish Americans

Uriah Phillips Levy
Ernestine L. Rose
Louis D. Brandeis
Lillian D. Wald

BY ALBERTA EISEMAN
Illustrated by Herb Steinberg

Zenith Books
Doubleday & Company, Inc.
Garden City, New York
1976

ISBN: 0-385-01588-7 Zenith Hardbound
       0-385-09662-3 Zenith Paperbound
Library of Congress Catalog Card Number 75–21224
The Zenith Books edition, published simultaneously in hardbound and paperback volumes, is the first publication of *Rebels and Reformers*.

For Alfred

Contents

Firebrand in the Navy

Uriah Phillips Levy

1792–1862

Uriah Phillips Levy, 1792–1862.

DAWN WAS BREAKING as the *New Jerusalem* left its mooring and sailed out into the Delaware River with the tide. A boy stood at the rail of the two-masted schooner, watching the sails fill with the morning breeze, admiring the practiced motions of the crew as they went about their routine. Soon, he thought, he would be working alongside them, very soon. He was a dark-haired, wiry ten-year-old, tall for his age. He turned toward the Philadelphia shore, taking a farewell look at all the ships moored in the harbor on this spring day in 1802. Behind hundreds of masts, he could still see the riverfront house he had left in the dark some hours before.

By candlelight he had stuffed into a canvas bag several blankets, heavy wool trousers and flannel shirts, a knife, two pairs of boots, and some school books. He had written a note, telling his parents that he was running away to sea, and would write again from the first port of call. Then he had tiptoed down the stairs and out of the three-story brick house that had been home all his life.

On the wall next to the front door hung the mezuzah, a Hebrew scroll held in a metal case, symbolizing, in the Jewish religion, God's careful watch over the house. The boy touched it lightly, then kissed the tips of his fingers, as he was taught to do since earliest childhood upon entering or leaving home. Then he slung the duffel bag over his shoulder, and resolutely walked down Front Street toward the dock where the *New Jerusalem* was moored.

Years later Uriah Phillips Levy would write of his regret at "putting my mother in such a worry, and making my father suffer." But as he watched Philadelphia disappear in the distance on that morning, the new cabin boy felt no qualms. He wanted above all things to be a sailor; since he was five years old he had haunted the wharves and shipyards near his home. The sea and ships cast a spell over him which would continue throughout his long, eventful life.

If Uriah missed the comforts of his parents' home, he never said so. He gladly carried out his duties as cabin boy—cleaning the cabins, making the captain's bunk, serving meals, scrubbing the pots and pans. When he had free time he went up on deck and the sailors taught him how to polish brightwork, scrub the deck, furl and reef the sails. He slept on a pile of sails in a corner of the forecastle, shared the crew's meals of salted meat, hard bread, codfish, rice, and potatoes. The only thing he would not eat was pork, which was forbidden by the Jewish religion. Some of the sailors made fun of him, but without malice; it was a small, friendly crew.

When Uriah had gone on board the *New Jerusalem* to apply for the post, he had told the captain that he could only sign on for two years. By that time, he explained, he would be twelve, the age at which a Jewish boy must start to study for his bar mitzvah, his formal initiation as a Jew. Captain James Wilkins had never known any seagoing Jews; there were not many Jews in the United States at that time—3,500 out of a population of some six million people. He had been impressed by the boy's independent spirit, by his knowledge of ships, by his fierce pride in his country and his religious faith. Since it was not unusual for cabin boys to sign on at an early age, the captain hired him, and told him to bring along his books, so he could help him learn some navigation in his spare time.

For two years Uriah sailed up and down the Atlantic seaboard, while the schooner carried cargoes of cotton from Georgia, tobacco from the Carolinas, lumber and sperm oil from New England ports. A few months before his thirteenth birthday he returned to his home and devoted himself to studying Hebrew and the writings of learned Jews, in preparation for his bar mitzvah.

On the Saturday after his thirteenth birthday, Uriah stood beside the rabbi in the synagogue, read a portion of the Bible in Hebrew, and delivered a well-rehearsed address. By the laws of Judaism he was then no longer a child but a man, a full member of the congregation. Having discharged his obligation, he then announced to his astonished parents that he was ready to go back to sea.

Michael and Rachel Levy tried to argue. They had always assumed their son would one day work in his father's shop on Market Street. They knew the importance of the merchant fleet to the young country, knew that American ships opened up vast areas of trade, sailing to Europe and to China, to Africa and the Caribbean Sea. But they were worried about storms and shipwrecks and the British fleet, which sometimes seized American vessels and their crews.

Uriah was a devoted son, but in any contest his passion for the sea would always win. It was decided that he would apprentice to a local shipowner to learn more about the sailor's trade. For the next five years he sailed on merchant vessels that carried cargoes of

molasses and rum, pineapples and salt pork. He learned
to climb the rigging, to take the wheel, to unload
cargo, to buy and sell with a sharp eye for profit.
During periods of time when no shipboard duty was
available he attended navigation school in Philadelphia
and took courses in sailing theory and chart making,
mathematics, and astronomy. By the time he was seventeen years old he held the rank of second mate on the
ship *Polly and Betsy*.

Loaded with lumber, the *Polly and Betsy* sailed toward the British West Indies in April of 1809, anchor-
ing in the harbor of Tortola. For several days Uriah
was busy with duties aboard ship, supervising the
unloading of the cargo. When that was done, the captain ordered him ashore to arrange for supplies of food
for the return voyage.

Uriah had looked forward to some time ashore; the
main streets of the lovely island were crowded with
seamen from a dozen different countries, with local laborers, and with officers from warships anchored in
the harbor. He carried out the ship's business, then
bought several hundred pounds of island sugar to sell
later, on his return to the United States. In those days
a young man working on a merchant vessel was allot-
ted a certain amount of space for his own cargo and
was entitled to trade for himself.

At the end of the day, Uriah sat relaxing in a tav-
ern when a man rushed in, shouting that a British
press gang was coming. Chairs were pushed back and
tables overturned as men fled through the back door;
Uriah sipped his coffee, unconcerned. He knew, of
course, that seamen often were kidnapped and forced to
serve in the British navy almost as slaves. To avoid it,

one needed protection papers, testifying to citizenship and place of birth; Uriah had his, securely wrapped in a money belt worn around his waist. He felt no need to worry.

A British sergeant in blue coat and white breeches stood before him. "Your name and papers!" he demanded bluntly.

Uriah stood. "Uriah Phillips Levy, American. Second mate on the brig *Polly and Betsy*." He took the papers from his money belt and handed them to the sergeant.

"You don't look like an American to me," the sergeant growled. "You look like a Jew."

"I am an American and a Jew," Uriah answered, thrusting out his chin.

The sergeant looked over the papers, then handed them back with a sneer. "If the Americans have Jew peddlers manning their ships, it's no wonder they sail so badly."

Another man might have seen he was outnumbered and kept his temper. Uriah struck the sergeant in the jaw. In seconds, a rifle butt hit him from behind, and he fell to the floor unconscious.

When he came to hours later, he was in the brig of the warship *Vermyra;* a British sailor stood over him, ordering him to get up. He was marched to the main deck with several others. Looking around, he could see his own ship, *Polly and Betsy*, anchored nearby, and yet he knew that if he tried to jump overboard he might be shot. A British officer approached, holding a Bible.

"You will be sworn into His Majesty's Navy," he said. "Remove your caps and raise your right hand."

Uriah stepped forward. "Sir, I cannot take the oath," he said firmly. "I am an American and I cannot swear allegiance to your king. And I am a Hebrew, and I do not swear on your testament or with my head uncovered."

The lieutenant had never been addressed in such proud fashion. Whether he liked the young man's spunk or perhaps because he had never known another Jew, he did not force him to swear. He told him he'd have to work or starve. Meanwhile, his case would be reviewed.

For several weeks, while the *Vermyra* sailed toward Jamaica, Uriah slaved as a deck hand, dreading the prospect of years in the British navy. Treatment was harsh, and the food almost inedible; he noticed that the crew was sullen and produced sloppy work. It started him thinking about conditions on both British and American ships, a concern which would grow in later years.

Once the ship reached Jamaica, Uriah was permitted an audience with the admiral, Sir Alexander Cochrane, the same man who some years later, during the War of 1812, would order the city of Washington put to the torch. To Uriah he was polite and fair. He checked his papers, said he disapproved of forcing Americans to serve in the British navy, and ordered him released, provided he could make his way back to the United States on his own.

After a while Uriah found a berth as a sailor on a merchantman headed for Boston; a month later he was back in Philadelphia, more devoted to the sea than before. His ambition was some day to own a ship; by the time he was nineteen, in 1811, he had saved enough to become one-third owner of a new 138-ton schooner, the *George Washington*.

At that time, he later wrote in his memoirs, he had "already passed through every grade of service—cabin boy, ordinary seaman, able-bodied seaman, boatswain, third, second and first mates, to that of captain. . . . I had become familiar with every part of my profession," he continued with confidence, "from the sculling of a jolly boat to the navigation of the largest vessel . . . from the splicing of a rope . . . to the heaving [to] of a ship in a gale of wind."

His pride in his first ship did not last long; on its first journey, to the Canary and the Cape Verde Islands, while Uriah was ashore on business, the *George Washington* was stolen by two mutinous members of the crew, who later sank it. Uriah was determined to find and punish the guilty men. He pursued them half way around the world and succeeded in having them arrested. While he awaited the outcome of their trial, war broke out between Britain and the United States, for the second time in half a century.

The War of 1812 was fought over an issue Uriah understood only too well: the right of American ships to sail the seas free from British interference. He could have chosen to serve aboard a privateer, a privately owned ship fighting alongside the nation's navy, and that way he might have earned considerable money. He decided instead to join the United States Navy as a sailing master. It only paid $40 a month, but it offered him, he later wrote, "the best proof of love to my country." For Uriah Phillips Levy, the right to wear the uniform of the United States in time of war was the best possible reward.

Uriah's first wartime assignment was in New York Harbor. He enjoyed the lively social life, yet going to dances and strolling with elegant young ladies along Battery Walk was not the kind of service he had in mind. He heard rumors that the Navy brig *Argus*, moored nearby, would be sailing for Europe in defiance of Britain's blockade of American harbors.

"Knowing that the cruise of the *Argus* could not fail to be a stirring one," he later wrote, "and hoping she might meet the enemy in . . . battle," Uriah borrowed a boat, rowed himself over, and offered his services to the commander, Captain William Henry Allen. His hopes were granted. The *Argus* was a small ship, but she carried more guns than any vessel her size in the Navy, and her exploits during the War of 1812 made naval history.

The *Argus'* first assignment in June 1813, was to transport America's new minister to France, William H. Crawford. After a battle during which a British schooner burned and sank, Mr. Crawford was deposited on the French coast. In Paris he would enlist France's assistance as peacemaker between the two nations at war. During the voyage the minister and the young sailing master became friends; many years later, he would come to Uriah's aid in time of trouble.

After Crawford's departure, Captain Allen described to his enthusiastic crew their next assignment. The *Argus* had been picked to be a raider, to strike at coastal settlements in Britain and to attack and destroy enemy ships in their own waters. All through the summer the *Argus* carried out this dangerous mission, until her name struck fear in the hearts of British sailors. Often the fighting was so fierce that Captain

Allen had to order the decks spread with wet sand, so his men would not slip on blood spilled in the battle. Finally the British navy declared all out war on the "phantom raider" and captured her. The *Argus'* captain sustained such serious wounds that he died, as did many of his men; the survivors were carried off to one of England's most dreaded jails. Levy was not aboard the *Argus* at the time of its final battle: he had been assigned to take another ship to France. He too was captured, and sent to the same prison.

Dartmoor Prison was known as "a tomb for the living"; the winter of 1813–14, the first the *Argus'* crew endured within its walls, was the coldest England had in fifty years. Snow was as high as five feet for many months, and food supplies, always scarce, often did not arrive at all. The barracks were unheated; windows let in the icy winds. Tough sailors though they were, many of the Americans fell ill and died; others gave in to apathy and despair.

Uriah Levy learned that keeping busy was the only way to survive the ordeal. From Frenchmen captured in previous battles, he took lessons in French and in fencing; he read endlessly the one navigation book he had salvaged from his ship. He memorized data on the construction and the handling of vessels, on distances, speeds, and charts; in turn, he taught all this to others. His active mind and his strong faith kept him alive during the sixteen months of imprisonment and cruel treatment. Finally he was released in an exchange of British and American prisoners. By then, the war was over.

Back in Philadelphia, family and friends advised Uriah not to continue his Navy service in peacetime.

Uriah's father had died during his absence; he would
have to support his mother and his young sisters and
brothers on the small salary of sailing master. Besides,
several people warned him of the prejudice he might
face.

"Nine out of ten of your superiors may not care a
fig that you are a Jew," wrote a friend, "but the tenth
may make your life a hell." Uriah knew the warning
was justified, but stood his ground. "What will be the
future of the Navy," he wrote back, "if others such as
I refuse to serve because of the prejudices of a few?
There will be other Hebrews, in times to come, of
whom America will have need."

He was equally loyal to his country and his religion;
he wanted to break ground for other Jews. But he had
chosen a branch of the service that drew its officers
from the ranks of wealth and privilege, the branch
that was most tradition-bound. He would battle against
that tradition for the rest of his life.

His first peacetime assignment was on the warship
Franklin, moored in the Philadelphia Navy Yard for
repairs. It was not the kind of challenging service Uriah
dreamed of during his months in prison, yet he did enjoy
it for a while. In his home town he was considered a war
hero; the glamour of his uniform, his dark good looks
and proud bearing brought him invitations to many
parties and balls. It was at such an affair that his first
clash with Navy establishment took place.

On a lovely June evening in 1816, Uriah Levy was
dancing with "a most beautiful young lady"—so said
the papers the next day—at the Patriots' Ball, when he
collided with William Potter, one of the officers from

the *Franklin*. Uriah assumed it was an accident and apologized.

Lieutenant Potter glared and remarked loudly that he hoped Uriah might be a better navigator at sea than on the dance floor. A little later Potter bumped him again; once more Uriah held his tongue, unwilling to make a scene in public. Then it happened a third time. Uriah whirled around and slapped the lieutenant across his face.

"You damned Jew!" Potter shouted in fury.

Uriah struck his most haughty pose and replied coolly: "That I am a Jew I neither deny, nor regret."

Within seconds a crowd gathered around them; several officers led Potter away, murmuring that their friend had had too much to drink. Uriah bowed to his flustered partner and continued to dance, hoping that the incident was over. But it was not; the following morning aboard ship, a friend of Potter's knocked at the door of Uriah's cabin, carrying a challenge to a duel.

Dueling was supposed to be illegal by 1816, but in the Navy it was the thing to do. Uriah wanted no part of it. He had hoped to be "the first Jew to rise to high rank in the Navy, not the first . . . killed in a duel." Yet he knew he would be called a coward if he refused.

The two men chose pistols as their weapons, named their seconds, invited along a group of friends. The day they chose was the twenty-first of June; before the duel the referee asked the two men if there was anything they wished to say. Uriah asked permission to recite a Hebrew prayer. Then, in a last attempt to avoid bloodshed, he announced he would not fire at his opponent, "although I am a crack shot."

"Coward!" Potter called out.

"You're a fool," Uriah replied.

The referee stepped between them. "Very well, gentlemen. No further words."

The adversaries faced each other grimly, twenty paces apart. Potter fired first, in haste, and missed his mark. Levy raised up his arm and fired into the air. Potter reloaded, but again failed to hit. Once more Uriah shot over his head. By then Potter was so angry he could no longer aim. Four times he missed, while Uriah continued to shoot into the air.

"Gentlemen, stop him, or I must!" he cried to Potter's friends.

"Stand back!" Potter called out, livid with rage. "I mean to have his life!"

The fifth shot grazed Uriah's ear, drawing some blood. Uriah held his fire, hoping Potter would consider his honor satisfied; but no, the lieutenant was reloading his gun.

"Very well," cried Uriah, taking aim for the first time. "I'll spoil his dancing." He may have meant to hit him in the leg, but the bullet struck Potter in the chest, and he fell to the ground. The doctor rushed over to his side. Potter was dead.

For weeks the duel was the talk of Philadelphia. There was much praise for Uriah's bravery and restraint, yet he had killed a man; for this, he was indicted by a grand jury.

The referee at the duel, the physician, several spectators, all testified; after a brief deliberation the jury acquitted him, with the foreman rising to say that "any man brave enough to fire in the air and let his opponent take deadly aim at him, deserves his life."

No sooner was Uriah acquitted than he was embroiled in new controversy. The "tempest in the coffee cups," as it became known, started aboard the *Franklin* on a calm Sunday morning when Sailing Master Levy, finding the breakfast table cluttered with used coffee cups, asked one of the mess boys to clean up. Lieutenant Francis Bond, the mess officer, objected that Uriah had no right to give orders to the cabin boy. Uriah replied that he had not given orders; Bond called him a liar; Uriah accused him of being a dictator. It took several men to keep them from coming to blows.

"You're a damn Jew!" Bond shouted as he left the wardroom. Then he filed charges against Uriah P. Levy for "ungentlemanly and unofficer-like conduct." There followed a court-martial—a Navy trial—at which testimony was presented on how many cups were on the table and whether they were tea or coffee cups; about who accused whom of what and what everyone wore on that ill-fated morning. The participants took it all with gravity, and Uriah made a fiery speech to the court which mentioned patriotism, honor, duty, and friendship. The case ended quickly, with a reprimand to both men for their behavior. Nothing more.

Meanwhile Uriah had taken an ambitious step. He had applied for a commission in the Navy under a rule that stated "[sailing] masters of extraordinary merit, and for extraordinary services, may be promoted to lieutenant." Friends advised him to wait before applying, in view of his recent encounters with the law, but Uriah had little use for patience. It turned out that his confidence was well placed: in March of 1817 he was commissioned a lieutenant, becoming the first Jewish officer ever to choose a lifetime career in the Navy of the United States.

Wearing the gold-fringed epaulets that marked his new rank, Uriah went to pose for Thomas Sully, one of the foremost painters of his time. The portrait Sully painted shows Uriah, at twenty-five years of age, in full dress uniform, his arms folded across his chest. It made him seem, it was said at the time, "a little vain, more than a little handsome, and very determined."

And so he was, a man of great intelligence and talent, proud of his background, but sensitive to a fault to any slight, be it intended or not. And in the Navy, his chosen proving ground, ability counted far less than influence and position. Few men ever became officers from sailing master, as he had; if they did, they were resented as intruders by those Levy described as coming "from the drawing room, with ruffled [shirts], perfumed locks and white kid gloves."

On his first assignment as lieutenant, he was cold-shouldered from the very start. Even before he was due to report to the frigate *United States* its captain, William Crane, had written to the commodore to complain that Lieutenant Levy had a reputation for being a "disturbing influence" and that his presence would create "disharmony" aboard ship. Uriah was ordered to report anyway. When he did, Captain Crane did not even look up from his desk, but coldly said "The *United States* has as many officers as I need or want."

It was unheard of for a ship's captain to disobey superior orders; yet it took three official letters before Captain Crane accepted Levy on his staff. When finally he was ushered into the captain's cabin after waiting outside for two hours, the captain did not rise, shake hands, or offer any of the courtesies that Navy protocol normally required.

Such was Uriah's welcome on the ship that was to be his home for sixteen months. Fortunately the executive officer, Thomas Catesby Jones, was fair and friendly and made sure that the other officers were civil to the newcomer.

It was in 1818, while the *United States* was cruising in the Mediterranean Sea, that Uriah Levy witnessed his first flogging. It was a frequent punishment in the navies of all countries in the 1800s; a few dozen lashes with a cat-o'-nine-tails were thought to be the best way to maintain discipline on board. A cruel captain could interpret regulations in such a way as to flog a man for any offense: for drinking, spitting on deck, or looking sullen when addressed by an officer.

On the *United States*, Captain Crane insisted that his entire crew witness each flogging. The cry, "All hands witness punishment, ahoy!" rang out early one morning before breakfast a few weeks after Uriah had come on board. A gunner's mate named Martin had returned from shore leave drunk and abusive and was to be given thirty lashes; by the rules of the day, that was moderate punishment.

Martin was tied to a wooden rack set up on deck, naked above the waist, his arms spread out, his wrists tied to the framework. While Captain Crane called out directions, the boatswain stepped up behind the prisoner, spread out his feet for balance and proceeded with his work. He was an expert; he could direct his blows in a precise crisscross pattern, so that no square

For forty years, Uriah Phillips Levy pursued his naval
career swinging from high honors to courts-martial.

inch of flesh was left untouched. The lash whistled through the air; each time it hit Martin's back blood spurted and his entire body jerked in pain. Several times during the beating Martin fainted; each time, a bucket of salt water was poured on him, he revived, and the beating continued. Finally the count of thirty was reached; the unconscious man was cut down from the rack and carried to his bunk, where the ship's surgeon would administer healing ointment to his wounds.

Uriah was sickened. For days he could talk of nothing else but the brutality and senselessness of physical punishment. It did not reform a man, Uriah argued, merely turned him against all authority. Besides, he told his fellow officers at mealtimes, it was a relic of British days; United States sailors were free men and should not be whipped like slaves.

The other officers mocked his passionate words. How could a captain ever control the crew without the threat of whipping? Behind his back they whispered that Uriah was a rebel, a troublemaker who disapproved of Navy policy. When he announced that if he ever had command of a ship he would throw overboard all whips and lashes, everyone laughed. Most officers on the *United States* did not believe Uriah would manage to remain in the Navy, much less command a ship.

Only the second-in-command sided with Levy. After some months, Catesby Jones was transferred; the new executive officer was hostile to Uriah from the start. A minor incident, in which Uriah lost his temper and slapped an enlisted man across the cheek, became grounds for another court-martial. Uriah was charged with disobedience to orders, contempt of a superior, and conduct unbecoming his rank. The presiding officer of the court was Captain Crane, and he had not forgotten that Lieutenant Levy had been forced on him. Uriah was found guilty on all charges and sentenced to be dismissed from the *United States.*

Such severe punishment over a minor incident was most unusual: when the case was reviewed by the fleet's commander in chief, Uriah's luck took a turn for the better, and the sentence was reversed. By that time, Uriah was so upset by the hostility and suspicion around him, that he was soon in trouble once again, over a matter even less important. He had an argument with a fellow officer, harsh words were exchanged, and Levy, in a fury, shouted to anyone who would listen that Lieutenant Williamson was a "poltroon, coward and scoundrel," as well as "rogue and rascal." He even took the trouble to go ashore—the *United States* was anchored in a harbor in Sicily at the time—and repeat the charges in various taverns frequented by the American fleet. Williamson preferred charges, and court-martial number three was under way.

This time, Uriah Phillips Levy was accused of "scandalous conduct, tending to the destruction of good morals," and of "being addicted to the vice of lying." He attempted to show he had not lied, that the incident had arisen from a misunderstanding. He tried to explain he was the victim of his fellow officers' hostility—"I have been designated in the language of idle scorn 'the Jew'!" he said dramatically. He finished with a passionate attack on anti-Semitism. The court was not impressed; it found him guilty and sentenced him to be dismissed from the Navy.

At twenty-seven years of age, after only seven years

in the uniform of his country, Uriah Levy had been
kicked out in disgrace. Spring of 1819 was the beginning of the saddest period of his life. He would not
go back to Philadelphia and face his friends and family; he spent most of his time in self-imposed exile in
France. For two years little is known of his activities.
Then, in one of those amazing turns of events that dot
Levy's career, he was suddenly back in the United
States. The proceedings of the 1819 court-martial had
reached the White House for the customary review
and President James Monroe, finding them unfair,
reversed them. "Although Lt. Levy's conduct merited
censure," wrote the President in 1821, "it is considered
that his long suspension from the service has been a
sufficient punishment for his offense. The sentence of
the court is therefore disapproved, and he is returned
to duty."

By then, everyone in the Navy had heard of the
"terrible-tempered Lieutenant Levy." His reputation
followed him everywhere he went, and he found himself challenged and goaded into repeated fights. He had
true friends, some of them in high office, yet he
aroused fierce hostility; for forty years this proud, vain
man pursued his career swinging from high honors to
courts-martial. Trouble and adventure seemed to follow him wherever he went.

His first command was that of a small, three-masted
bark named the *Revenge*. On his way toward boarding
his new ship in Charleston, South Carolina, Uriah
witnessed a devastating tornado, and at great peril to
himself managed to rescue an entire family. He assumed
command of the *Revenge* with his arm in a sling, and
his new crew welcomed him aboard as a hero. His tri-

umph was short-lived; cruising in the Caribbean, the *Revenge* soon hit a storm and was shipwrecked.

His next assignment, in 1823, was as a lieutenant on the *Cyane*, a frigate sailing the South Atlantic Ocean. On a day when the ship was being repaired in the harbor of Rio de Janeiro, Uriah happened to be walking along the wharf when he saw two Americans, a sailor and a midshipman, fighting against a dozen Brazilians.

"What's happening here?" he asked.

"American seaman, sir," replied the midshipman, "escaping impressment."

"Then we'll save him!"

Remembering his own forced service years before, Uriah jumped into the fight, fists flying. He was gashed by a Brazilian bayonet, but he fought on and managed to carry the young sailor back to safety on the *Cyane*.

The rescued seaman sang Uriah's praises to the crew, the captain shook his hand; once more, Uriah was a hero. The next day, a barge rowed by a dozen men approached the *Cyane*. A man in splendid uniform addressed Uriah, who had been supervising some work on deck; it was Dom Pedro, Emperor of Brazil. He pointed to Uriah's bandaged arm. Speaking in French, he asked if it was he who had rescued the American seaman the previous day. Uriah acknowledged that it was, fearing his act might have angered the Brazilian ruler.

"Your rescue . . . was a courageous act," said the Emperor, as Uriah stood at attention. "I have ordered that no citizen of the United States is ever again to be impressed into the Brazilian navy."

Uriah was amazed. While officers and men stood by, unable to understand French, ·Dom Pedro inquired as to Uriah's wounds, his background, his training in seamanship. Then he proceeded to offer him the command of a new frigate, and the rank of captain if he would enter the Brazilian navy. The reply came without hesitation.

"Your Majesty, I must graciously decline this great honor," Uriah said in his most formal French. "I love my country and the Navy of the United States. With no reflection upon you, sir, or your service, I would rather serve as a cabin boy in the United States Navy than hold the rank of admiral in any other service in the world!"

For a brief while Uriah Levy enjoyed the admiration of his shipmates and the entire squadron. On his return to Philadelphia in 1828, however, he found that no new assignment was in sight. He was then thirty-six years old; he had been a lieutenant for eleven years. If prospects for a promotion seemed uncertain, it was not only because of his reputation as a hothead or his religion; in the 1830s the Navy was unsure about its plans. There were not enough ships and too many officers; many resigned rather than wait around for years for an assignment. The thought of leaving the Navy seems not to have occurred to Uriah Levy. When a friend suggested that he marry, settle down, and join him in business, Uriah replied, "I am married to the sea."

For ten years he saw no active service, but it was not wasted time. He made many visits to New York. Fascinated by the quick growth of that city, he made investments in real estate which accumulated a fair amount of wealth in a brief time. He never ceased to concern himself with naval matters; he traveled to Europe to study conditions in the navies of Great Britain and France, he studied new developments and wrote articles for magazines and journals.

He read a great deal, particularly about the career of his favorite hero, Thomas Jefferson. Such was his admiration for the author of the Declaration of Independence that he commissioned a statue by one of the great sculptors of the day, and presented it to the Congress; today it stands in the Capitol Rotunda. In 1836 he went on a pilgrimage to Monticello, which had been Jefferson's home; since his death ten years before, the house had passed through the hands of numerous owners. Finding it in shameful disrepair, Uriah bought it and began a long, costly program of restoring it in accordance with Jefferson's design.

The following year, while he was at work on the restoration, he received notice that he had been promoted a commander in the Navy. By then his real estate dealings had made him a wealthy man, and he surely did not need his Navy pay. Nevertheless he immediately applied for active duty and in 1838 was assigned to be commanding officer of the war sloop *Vandalia.*

When he arrived in Pensacola, Florida, to take command of his ship, he found it in sorry shape. Its hull was rotten, its twenty guns covered with rust. The crew was not much better: many men were addicted to liquor, the rest were petty criminals who had been transferred from other ships. Typically, Uriah Levy was undaunted. He worked with his crew to overhaul every inch of the *Vandalia;* five months later, in February of 1839, she was ready to sail out toward the Gulf of Mexico, trim and seaworthy, its guns painted bright blue.

Blue guns were not the only different touch on Levy's ship. From the first day he changed important rules. There would be no corporal punishment whatever on the *Vandalia*, he announced. His officers were astounded. They warned him that without the lash the men would not obey; mutiny would ensue. Uriah ignored them. He had waited years to put his theories into practice; he was convinced sailors would act responsibly if only they were treated as men rather than dogs. He posted a list of regulations and devised a series of unusual penalties to enforce them. A man guilty of stealing would have to wear a wooden sign around his neck that said *thief*; someone drunk on duty would wear one marked *a drunkard's punishment.* He was sure that ridicule would have the desired effect.

When a young sailor named John Thompson was accused of mocking an officer by mimicking his voice, Uriah ordered that a small dab of tar be applied to his bare buttocks, and some bird feathers be affixed to the tar.

"If you are going to act like a parrot, you should look like one," the commander decreed. The sailors roared with laughter, and Thompson himself admitted that a few minutes' embarrassment was better than the lash. Yet this unique punishment was to haunt Uriah later on.

By the time the *Vandalia* returned to Florida at the end of a fourteen-month cruise, the crew was well trained and efficient, with high regard for their captain. Yet Uriah's unorthodox methods and his concern for his sailors had irked the officers; Lieutenant George Hooe was so outspoken in his criticism, and disobedient, that he was dismissed from the squadron, and reprimanded.

On the ship's return, talk of Uriah's unusual disciplinary methods had spread throughout the naval base. Several newspapers commended Uriah Levy for his enlightened, forward-looking views. Yet the older officers in the Navy thought him a radical who would disgrace the service. And though he had expected to be sent out to sea again right away, Uriah was told to "await orders." He wrote to Washington for clarification, but there was no reply. He went back to New York to "await orders," taking with him a gift from his loyal crew, a model of the *Vandalia*.

It was two years before he heard from the Navy, and when he did, in 1842, it was a brief note ordering him to appear before a court-martial for "forgery, cowardice, and cruel and scandalous conduct." His accuser was George Mason Hooe, the lieutenant dismissed from the *Vandalia*, who had spent the intervening months plotting revenge. The major charge stemmed from the punishment of John Thompson.

At the trial the incident was made out to be a full-fledged tar-and-feathering; it was claimed that the sailor had been left in shock. Uriah countered that "a dab of tar no larger than a silver dollar" had been applied to the young man's rear end for a few minutes. He knew he had broken no rule and thought at most he would be admonished not to repeat this form of punishment. The verdict was a total shock: he was found guilty and dismissed from the Navy.

Defeated and depressed, Uriah thought his career in the Navy was finished for good. Once more, his fortunes turned. When President John Tyler read the records of Levy's court-martial, he concluded that the punishment had been out of proportion to the crime. Pointing out that "no harm was done to the person" of the sailor, he modified Uriah's sentence to twelve months' suspension from the Navy. In June 1844, when a letter arrived promoting him from commander to captain, Uriah was overjoyed. Surely this meant his past mistakes had been forgiven, his talents recognized. He knew the Navy was not involved in any wars, that few new ships were being built, yet he had hopes that he would soon be assigned a command. He ordered a new, resplendent uniform, and awaited an official call.

Meanwhile, his many ventures kept him busy. He paid frequent visits to his Virginia home, working to bring Monticello back to the style and beauty of Jefferson's day. He wrote on naval matters, on steam-powered ships, on improved education for seamen, and, above all, on the abolition of the lash. He dashed off numerous letters to newspapers in Philadelphia, New York, and Washington, D.C., calling the Navy's use of flogging a "barbarous" and "medieval" punishment. Then he took to the lecture platform, holding audiences spellbound with descriptions of human flesh being sliced to shreds, of the victim's groans.

Gradually, his crusade found support in the Congress. The senator from New Hampshire, John P. Hale, introduced a bill to end corporal punishment in the Navy. Debate continued on the Hill for many months, with Uriah furnishing details and data to friendly legislators. At one point he even distributed dozens of cat-o'-nine-tails, so members of Congress could test them on their own skin. Finally, in September 1850, a bill passed limiting the use of the lash; a few years later it was outlawed for good.

Uriah was elated by the news. In the press he was hailed as the "father of the abolition of flogging," although he was the first to acknowledge the vital help of Senator Hale. "My humble share in this work of humanity and patriotism," he later wrote in his memoirs, "will ever be a spring of joy and consolation of which I cannot be deprived by persecution or injustice."

It was a moment of personal triumph, but it did not serve to endear him to the Navy. At one and the same time he was attacking Navy traditions, yet pleading to be assigned to a command. The Navy establishment considered him a rebel and a crank; replies to his applications for active duty grew constantly more chilly. Sometimes he received no acknowledgment at all. Through it all, his yearning for the sea did not abate. He would spend many hours on the New York waterfront sitting on a bench and gazing at the warships in the bay, the clipper ships tied at the dock and the ferries plying to Brooklyn and New Jersey.

In the fall of 1853, at sixty-one, Uriah startled family and friends by marrying a girl of eighteen, Virginia Lopez. She was his niece, from the West Indies; when they met, she had been left penniless on her father's death. He would marry her to protect her, Uriah said.

Virginia was short and pretty, a good dancer, fluent in Spanish and French. Surely the marriage brought new zest to his life. Still, he continued to solicit the Navy for a command. Then in September 1855 a letter came, delivering to Uriah the most shocking blow of his career. "To promote the efficiency of the Navy," he read, two hundred officers were to be stricken from the rolls. Uriah Phillips Levy was to be one of them.

Never one to give up, Uriah inquired as to whether any of the other officers was planning to challenge the decision. Nobody was. Almost sixteen years had passed since he had held active duty. He was sixty-three, with a lovely young wife, two splendid houses, and a fortune to enjoy. Most men would gladly have resigned themselves to that lot. But the passage of time had not made Uriah Levy less of a fighter. He swore he would redeem his name and launched what one newspaper called "one of the greatest fights for justice in the annals of the armed forces."

Uriah hired one of the finest lawyers in the country, Benjamin Butler. Together, the two men drafted a petition more than 9,000 words long, arguing that the Naval Review Board had overstepped the authority granted it by Congress. They maintained that the Navy had three major objections to Uriah: that he had risen through the ranks, that he was outspoken in his hatred of corporal punishment, and that he was a Jew. It was the first time in the nation's history that anti-Semitism had been openly discussed in the Congress; before that, the official assumption had been that prejudice did not exist in the land.

It took a year before Congress agreed to set up a court of inquiry to hear the case of the officers who had been dismissed. In November 1857 the last fight

between Uriah Phillips Levy and the Navy of the
United States began. The Navy introduced a string of
officers to testify that Uriah was "incompetent,
unreliable," and "generally disliked." In reply, the
defense presented witnesses of its own: thirteen officers
on active duty and six retired, who testified to his excellent qualities of leadership. "Levy was liked by all
but the anti-Semites," said an officer who had served
under him.

Then came a parade of acquaintances and friends
from every business and profession, mayors and con-
gressmen, bank presidents and doctors, Christians and
Jews. Seventy-five people took their turn on the stand
to speak in favor of Uriah Phillips Levy and against
the Navy's treatment of him. Finally, more than
a month after the opening of the hearings, Levy took
up his own defense. With military bearing, in a voice
as strong as ever, Levy read a plea for justice that
took four days to complete. He went back over his
young days in the service, his patriotism, his ambition,
his desire to make the Navy more humane, his upbringing and religous faith, his struggle against bigotry.
Then on December 22, he concluded: "What is my
case today, if you yield to this injustice, may tomor-
row be that of the Roman Catholic or the Unitarian
. . . There is but one safeguard, and this is to be
found in an honest, wholehearted, inflexible support
of the wise, the just, the impartial guarantee of the
Constitution. I have the fullest confidence that you
will faithfully adhere to this guarantee, and therefore,
with like confidence, I leave my destiny in your
hands."

"It was," commented a Washington paper, "one of

the most glorious pleas ever made in the history of the United States Navy: a plea that 'right should be done'!" and it was greeted, as Levy sat down, by an enthusiastic burst of applause from the audience. The court's verdict was unanimous. It found Uriah Phillips Levy to be "morally, mentally, physically and professionally fit for the Naval Service and . . . ought to be restored to the active list of the Navy."

Now the Navy tried to make amends as best it could. Though he was sixty-five and had not seen active service for seventeen years, Uriah was respectfully requested to take command of the sloop *Macedonian* and sail her to join the Mediterranean fleet. Uriah replied he would be honored. Then he added an unheard of request. Since his wife was "an orphan," he wrote, "and not a native of this country, without any protection during my absence," he sought permission to take her on board.

Uriah's luck was running at flood tide; the Navy assented. The aging warrior and his young wife shared a cabin as the *Macedonian* cruised from port to port. On board, some of the officers were dismayed at finding the Captain's cabin cluttered with "hoops and skirts, bonnets and shoes." "She seems determined to show off her dresses," a critical midshipman wrote. Ashore, Captain and Mrs. Levy were received by European diplomats and kings.

In 1860 he was given the rank of commodore, then the Navy's highest rank, and placed in command of the entire Mediterranean fleet. Forty-three years after his first commission, he stood at attention on the deck of his ship, while the fleet fired a thirteen gun salute. He had at last achieved his true ambition.

A few months later it was time to bring back part of the fleet to the United States, and he was ready to retire. Though he walked down the gang plank for the last time proud and erect, he was sixty-eight years old and he could feel it. He settled down with Virginia in the big house on St. Mark's Place in New York; when Civil War broke out in April 1861 he made one more brave gesture and offered his services to his country once again.

In November 1861 President Lincoln appointed him to head the court-martial board in Washington, D.C., but he was not able to carry out his duties for long. In early spring he caught a cold which developed into pneumonia; on March 22, 1862, Uriah Phillips Levy died.

Almost a century later the Navy dedicated a destroyer in his name in World War II. He would have been proud of the U.S.S. *Levy;* it was known as "a swift and deadly sub-killer."

In 1959 his name was honored once again when a chapel devoted to the Jewish faith was dedicated at the United States Naval Base in Norfolk, Virginia. The Chief of Chaplains opened the chapel with these words: "Uriah P. Levy, as a naval officer and a citizen, was a dominant person in the formative years of our nation. You have done well to name this chapel after him."

Crusader for Human Rights

Ernestine L. Rose

1810–1892

Ernestine L. Rose, 1810–1892.

Rabbi Potowski could not believe his daughter's words.

"Father, I will not marry him," Ernestine repeated, her black eyes flashing an indignant look.

"Why?" asked the rabbi. "He is a good man, a religious Jew. Is it because he is much older than you are?"

"It is because I do not love him, Father. He is a complete stranger to me."

The rabbi sighed. No other girl in Poland talked of love except his daughter; in 1826 a girl married the man her parents chose. Ernestine was sixteen; most girls her age had been married at least a year, many were mothers. He had made a good match for her, betrothed her to a respectable man, many years older and able to take good care of her. He tried once more.

"But the marriage contract is already signed!"

"I have not signed it, and I will not honor it." Her voice was firm and sure.

In the Jewish community in Piotrków, there was no one else who would defy the rabbi. He was the spiritual head of the community; everyone respected his wisdom and his learning. But Ernestine had followed her own will almost, it seemed, since the day she was born.

At the age of five she had begun to read; soon she was studying the Holy Book, refusing to believe that it was only for boys to study. Girls were supposed to learn to cook and sew. Then came the questions: "How was the universe *really* formed?" or "How did evil begin?"

Rabbi Potowski would answer her as best he could. If he was busy, he would sometimes say "little girls must not ask such questions."

"*Why* must little girls not ask such questions?" That statement disturbed Ernestine most of all. Even as a young child, she could not bear to think that there were questions she must not ask, areas that she must ignore. All through her life she would fight against such thinking.

"I was a rebel at the age of five," she wrote many years later. When she was five or six, her parents and their friends would smile and shake their heads as they recounted her latest headstrong saying. But as she grew older the smiles were replaced by disapproval and alarm. In their close-knit, traditional community there was no room for people who questioned authority.

In Piotrków, as in most of Eastern Europe, those of the Jewish faith lived separate lives, by royal decree and also by their own choice. When they ventured outside their section of the city on market day or if they had to travel to another town, they ran the risk of being attacked and beaten by Christians, sometimes killed. Not that they were entirely safe in their own ghetto. Periodically, organized massacres—pogroms—swept through the Jewish quarters. Often the pogroms were inspired by the emperor, the Tsar of all the Russias, sometimes by the Church. It did not take much to arouse the downtrodden Polish peasants, and the Jews were an easy target for their anger.

The Jewish population lived at the mercy of the Christian Polish majority, but Poland itself was far from free. The rulers of Austria, Prussia, and Russia had partitioned the country among themselves and ruled without pity for its people. The ghetto was like a prison in a prison.

This was the world in which Ernestine Louise Potowski was born on January 13, 1810. Probably she was given a different name at birth, but there are no records to that effect; Ernestine Louise is the name by which she wished to be known. She came into a world in which men and women born in the Jewish faith spent their entire lives hemmed in by regulations made by others; a world of struggle against oppressive laws and taxes, of poverty and no hope; a world of traditions closely held. All the disputes, conflicts, and troubles of the community were brought to the rabbi for his judgment; his young daughter, with her quick intelligence, listened to people's sorrows and felt them deeply.

For most Polish Jews, religious tradition was worn as a protective mantle, accepted gladly. But Ernestine Louise was not one to accept anything without question. After her mother's death, Rabbi Potowski found the burden of her upbringing ever heavier. He had hoped that marriage and motherhood would help to make her less defiant, but Ernestine would not bend.

She went to see the man to whom her father had betrothed her and asked him to release her from the engagement contract. Angry that anyone would turn him down, he refused. No, he would not return her inheritance, he added. It had been promised him as dowry.

What could Ernestine do? Normally, such a case would come before the rabbi for decision, but the rabbi's mind was made up. She would have to take the case before a Polish court, a step almost unheard of among Piotrków's Jews. It was a frightening decision, the most difficult she had ever had to take. She did not hesitate.

She hired a sleigh and driver and drove through high snows and howling winds for many hours, to the town where the regional tribunal met to hear disputes. All through the long, cold ride she thought about the trial that lay ahead. She would present her own case, she decided. Who else knew the circumstances as well as she? Finally she came before the judges, a young Jewish woman brave enough to stand before a Christian court, seeking the right to choose her own life mate. They were so impressed with her defense that they granted her the right to undo the marriage contract and retain her inheritance.

She was elated by the outcome of the trial, happy that justice had been done. On her way back she decided that she would turn the dowry over to her father: he had always taken good care of her, and she had no need of her own funds.

On her return several days later, she found that the rabbi had made a decision of his own. While she was gone he had taken a wife. Ernestine's new stepmother was barely her own age. Soon the sixteen-year-old bride took over the running of the house; Ernestine felt there was no room for her at home.

Increasingly, she also knew that she did not belong within the confines of the ghetto. Yet as a Jew, if she left Piotrków, she would not be allowed to choose where she would live. She yearned to read, to study, to explore the ways of other people; for that she would have to go abroad.

She took as much of her inheritance as she would

need for the first few weeks away from home and left the rest to be used to help the poor. Then she said good-by to her father and left Piotrków, never to return.

It is hard to picture what enabled a girl of seventeen, brought up in a small Polish town, in a ghetto, to find within herself the courage to leave home and head for a foreign capital. But she did. In 1827 she arrived in Berlin, one of the foremost cultural centers of the day. She may have thought she was leaving behind restraints and discrimination, but she soon found that in the German states Polish Jews were far from welcome. Restrictions were placed on their movement, on what kind of employment they could hold, on the length of their stay.

Shocked by the injustice of this, Ernestine wrote an indignant letter to the King of Prussia. She was granted an audience. Her argument must have been persuasive, because the King ruled she could remain as long as she liked and engage in any business she might wish. Now she had to find a way to earn a living and at the same time remain free to study and to travel, the very reasons for which she had left home.

Sitting in a rented room in Berlin, thinking about the possibilities ahead, she was often aware of unpleasant cooking odors that lingered in the house long after meals were finished. Might there not be some way to put an end to such smells? She thought about it, investigated various ideas, came up with the notion of a paper treated with chemicals which would dispel bad odors. Her invention was manufactured and sold well: most homes had poor ventilation in those days and needed deodorizing.

For the time being, her financial problems were over. Now she could do what she wanted: read freely, improve her knowledge of German, travel throughout the German states. During the next two years she also learned, with great sadness, that it was not only in her native land that people were exploited and oppressed.

She saw peasants and factory workers laboring fourteen hours a day and yet living in poverty. She saw university students thrown in jail for expressing the hope that their country might be free of tyranny. She saw Jewish people denied many rights that others held. So, at the age of nineteen, she left Berlin. By then she was a wiser, well-informed young woman, fluent in German, eager to move on to other countries to learn all she could about the human condition.

She spent some months in Holland, then in Belgium and France, not merely sightseeing, but involving herself in the social problems of each country. She heard that a revolt had broken out in Poland and she tried to get back, but was denied entry at the border. In 1830 she arrived in England, knowing she would find others there who shared her concerns and that there she might stay.

In the 1830s England was the cradle of social reform. The industrial revolution had its beginnings in Great Britain, creating fortunes for a few manufacturers and at the same time giving rise to an entirely new class of overworked, exploited laborers. Even as a newcomer, just starting to become familiar with the language, Ernestine gladly mingled with the workers who would come to hear speakers demanding higher wages, shorter hours, and the right to vote for the working man.

She was happy in London. She soon found work as a tutor in Hebrew and German, and she was able to earn a little more by selling the deodorizing paper she had invented. During a workers' meeting, she heard a speech by Robert Owen, one of the foremost social reformers of the day. As she listened, she found reflected in his words her own desire for individual freedom, for justice for humanity. The very principles she had been trying to express seemed basic to the Owenite philosophy. From that day, the young, idealistic Polish woman and the sixty-year-old British reformer began a lifelong friendship. He called her "my daughter"; she became one of his most dedicated disciples.

Owen believed that man was the product of his environment. Surround him with poor conditions, Owen felt, and man's thoughts and actions will be evil; surround him with good, he will be good. To prove his theory, Robert Owen had taken over the management of a cotton mill in New Lanark, Scotland, and made it an experimental community, with new homes and food stores, improved working conditions, and a school, one of the first for working-class children in the world. Owen traveled widely and lectured to rally support for his theories; he was so impressed with Ernestine's intelligence and convictions that he asked her to address a large meeting of London workers. Despite her halting English, Ernestine held the audience's attention and was rewarded with enthusiastic applause. It was the start of a career as public speaker that lasted forty years and spanned two continents.

Ernestine's friendship with Robert Owen was one of the most important influences in her life. She had inherited from her father the ability to dedicate herself totally to a faith; from Owen she inherited the faith to which she would devote her life. Under his auspices, she helped to found the Association of All Classes of All Nations, a pioneer group that stood for human rights for all people, regardless of sex, class, color, or country. The group accepted no formal religion, their spiritual goal being solely to make mankind "and all other living things, as happy as possible." By adopting this radical creed, Ernestine made a full break with the religion of her ancestors, a break she had begun to make when she left Piotrków. She would always consider herself "a daughter of poor, crushed Poland, and the downtrodden and persecuted people called the Jews." Formal religion and the traditional concept of God ceased to have any meaning for her.

Through her new friends, she met and fell in love with a young Englishman named William Ella Rose. He was a skilled jeweler and silversmith, a Christian, and, like her, a fervent disciple of Robert Owen. Soon after their marriage, Ernestine and William Rose set sail for the United States.

In May of 1836 the young couple landed in New York City. Almost ten years before, Ernestine had left her native Poland, broken with the past, started out on a journey of discovery, learning, searching for a philosophy that would express her ideals for mankind. It was natural that she would be drawn to the United States, the new country founded on the premise that all men are created equal. She was then twenty-six years old; William was twenty-three. Both were eager to be part of the growing, optimistic young nation.

They settled in New York City, at 484 Grand Street. The New York directory for the following year records that William Rose opened a silversmith shop in his home. He was an able and imaginative craftsman, and in time he built up a good following, but at the start, Ernestine used her ingenuity to help bring in some extra income. In Germany and England she had made and marketed her deodorizing paper; in the United States she manufactured her own brand of toilet water—Cologne water, it was called at the time.

The New York *Beacon* printed an item about the Roses in March 1838:

"Mrs. Rose, an interesting Polish lady of education and great accomplishments, and who is already partially known to the readers of the *Beacon*, from the part she has taken in some liberal public meetings, now manufactures Cologne and other German waters. . . . Mr. and Mrs. Rose keep a small Fancy and Perfumery store . . . he repairs jewelry, watches, ornaments and trifles which nobody else thinks of; while she manufactures German waters and offers them for sale, wholesale and retail, and for exportation, of course."

It did not take Ernestine long to become known in liberal circles in New York. There were many causes to which she was immediately drawn and a wide choice of meetings to attend. Three years before the Roses reached the United States, a small group of reformers meeting in Philadelphia had founded the American Anti-Slavery Society. They called themselves "abolitionists"; they pleaded, to a largely uncaring nation, the cause of liberty for the Negro slave.

Ernestine had never witnessed slavery at first hand. She had never seen black children torn from their mothers at an auction, never watched the overseer's whip slice across a man's back. Yet she had known enough of human servitude in other forms; within months of her arrival, she made the abolitionist cause her own.

Another crusade that soon took up her energy and time was that of rights for women. In the United States, she found out, women were not much better off than they were in Europe. During the administration of President Andrew Jackson the right to vote had been extended to include most men, if they were white, citizens of the United States, and over the age of twenty-one. Women had no legal rights of their own: they could not sue or be sued; they could not vote, yet they were obligated to pay taxes to help support a government in which they had no say. Before marriage, women were under the protection of their father; after marriage, that of their husband. If the marriage ended in divorce, the husband received custody of the property and of the children. Women were not admitted at most universities; if they ever worked outside the home, it was only because of economic necessity, and then they would be given the jobs with lowest pay.

Man had decreed that woman's world was in the home, "that scene of purest and dearest joy, home is the empire of woman. There she plans, directs, performs . . ." So said the most popular women's magazine of its day, *Godey's Lady's Book*. That recipe for female happiness did not reflect the feelings of Ernestine Rose nor of her husband, who fully shared her aspirations, nor of many American-born women, who had a different vision for themselves.

The very year that Ernestine Rose landed in New York, a resolution was introduced in the legislature of the state to investigate ways of improving the civil and property rights of married women. It was a mild resolution, but it was a start in the direction of upgrading woman's status. As soon as Ernestine read about the bill she drew up a petition in its favor and went from house to house asking other women to sign it. Surely, she thought, women would understand the benefits they would derive from such a law; as she knocked on doors in her neighborhood, the door was usually slammed in her face. If a man came to open, he would say that women had too many rights already and not enough work to do. Wives would echo their husband's words: "Indeed, we have rights enough!" many said.

In five months Ernestine managed to collect five signatures! She must have been discouraged, yet she did not let that stand in her way. She sent off the petition with five signatures to the legislature in Albany and then set out again to collect more in other parts of the city. She was convinced that by explaining to women their condition, "by holding before them the mirror of facts," she later wrote, she had "roused, to some extent at least, their dormant energies." She believed strongly in "rousing dormant energies." "'Agitate! Agitate!'" she used to say, "ought to be the motto of every reformer. Agitation is the opposite of stagnation—the one is life, the other, death."

It took twelve years before the bill was passed by the New York legislature, years during which she spoke in its behalf, collected thousands of signatures, and often traveled to Albany to testify about the need for such an act and the necessity to begin to update the status of women. In the state capital the bill aroused immediate opposition. It was argued that to grant married women legal rights separate from their husbands' would cause serious marital conflict and might even shatter the institution of marriage. It was sometimes whispered that such rights might lead women into a life of immorality and perhaps prostitution.

There were many women besides Ernestine Rose who mocked such arguments and worked hard for the bill's passage. One of them was Elizabeth Cady Stanton, another was Paulina Wright (later Davis); they befriended the energetic young reformer whose background was so very different from theirs. Together with Lucretia Mott of Philadelphia they became the guiding spirits of the new women's rights movement.

For Ernestine, the crusade for women was part of a much larger struggle for human rights. She joined a group of freethinkers who had organized a Society for Moral Philanthropists; they sponsored public lectures and debates on a large variety of topics. As many as two thousand people would attend if the topic was interesting and the speaker lively. Ernestine Rose became one of their most popular attractions. Often people would come not because they were interested in her ideas, but because of the novelty of a female speaker. Few women had the courage to express their opinions from a public platform at that time. The audience might have come to scoff, but her eloquence and her logic were such that many stayed to cheer. In the summer of 1837 she took part in a debate that continued for thirteen weeks, and several papers took notice of the debating skills of the "Polish lady." A few months later, she created a stir that brought her to the attention of a far wider audience.

In December 1837 a public meeting was called to find ways to improve the common schools, as public schools were then called. There was intense interest in the subject; five thousand people jammed the church where the gathering was held. A prominent minister from Kentucky, the Reverend Robert Breckenridge, rose to speak. He lamented the fact that out of four and a half million school age children in the United States, almost a million were deprived of education. Presently he left the topic and launched into an angry tirade against those godless people who dared to oppose the institution of slavery and advocated women's rights. "Infidels," he called them in scathing tones.

Ernestine was familiar with that word. Whenever anyone championed an unpopular cause, they were accused of "infidelity." She waited until Breckenridge had completed his speech, then she stood up. "Will the chairman permit me to ask the gentleman who has just closed a question in relation to his remark on infidelity?" she asked.

Everyone turned their head toward the gallery; there stood a young woman in an elegant dress, with her black hair in tight ringlets and her dark eyes calmly facing the chairman. It was unusual for a woman's voice to ring out in a public place; that she should dare to challenge a clergyman was so rare that for a moment everybody sat still. A female voice hissed out the words "Infidel! Infidel!" Then the storm broke. People shouted "Throw her out!" "Drag her outside!" There was hooting and stamping, hissing

Ernestine Rose and her crusading friends organized
hundreds of meetings and traveled thousands of miles
to rally support for women's rights and the abolition
of slavery.

and cursing. Through it all Ernestine quietly stood, waiting for the noise to die down so she could be recognized by the chair. When order finally returned, the minister replied, "The principles of my Christian religion forbid me to fight with a woman," and sat down, to a round of applause.

Many newspapers reported this exchange, convinced that when a woman dared to challenge the words of a clergyman, and in a church, the world was truly on the edge of chaos. Yet there were people who applauded her courage and requested that she address their groups. Before long she was much in demand by anti-slavery and women's rights groups, traveling at first within New York State, later all through the North and West and as far south as Kentucky and South Carolina. By mid-century, she was often called "Queen of the Platform."

"I look back to that time," she wrote many years later, "when a stranger, and alone, I went from place to place in the highways and byways, did the work and paid my bills with great pleasure and satisfaction."

She was not deterred by the hostility she often met. Some newspapers criticized her accent and manner of speaking, some went as far as to imply that she was a "foreign propagandist" whose activities were subsidized by "British gold." The Albany *Register* warned that unless "the outpourings of fanaticism and folly of this Polish propagandist" were halted, American institutions would collapse. She replied: "Everyone who ever advanced a new idea, no matter how great and noble, has been subjected to criticism . . . but it is quite certain that no true soul will ever be deterred from the performance of a duty by any criticism."

She had admirers as well as opponents. When she lectured in Michigan, the House of Representatives passed a resolution expressing praise for her eloquence and grace of delivery. A report on the status of women in Michigan, written much later, found that "the agitation on the subject of women's suffrage began in this state in 1846 with the advent of Ernestine L. Rose."

Her travels, lectures, and debates were regularly reported in the Boston *Investigator*, a free-thought weekly which published articles and letters from her. She was soon well known to social reformers throughout the United States. In 1845, when she attended the first national convention of Infidels—the word had been applied in derision, but reformers wore it as a badge of pride—she had a seat of honor next to her friend and teacher, Robert Owen, the seventy-four-year-old pioneer crusader for human rights. A newspaper opposed to their cause took a bow in her direction by calling her "the highly accomplished, talented and intellectually beautiful Mrs. Rose."

She worked in close association with William Lloyd Garrison and Frederick Douglass, leaders of the abolitionist movement, and such pioneers of women's rights as Frances Wright, Lucretia Mott, Paulina Wright, Sojourner Truth, and young Susan B. Anthony, who soon became one of Ernestine's closest friends.

The two crusades frequently overlapped during those years; the American woman's struggle for equality was born of her involvement in the anti-slavery fight. The first convention called by a group of women to promote their own rights took place in July 1848, in a small town in New York State called Seneca Falls. One hundred people, one third of them men, signed a resolution affirming "that it is the duty of the women of this country to secure to themselves their sacred right to the elective franchise."

It was considered a radical proposal, and the organizers of that first convention were attacked and vilified from editorial pages and pulpits. But for many women around the land, that gathering at Seneca Falls was a source of new hope and inspiration. Someone had finally begun to talk about what needed doing, at an open convention, unafraid. It was a bright beginning, but the road ahead was to be long and hard.

Ernestine Rose and her crusading friends organized hundreds of meetings and conventions; traveled endless miles in unheated, uncomfortable trains; wrote many speeches in their attempt to rally support for their cause; debated, argued, pleaded. Some gatherings were dignified and serious. Many more were broken up by rowdy and often violent demonstrations.

A meeting of the American Anti-Slavery Society in New York in 1850 was broken up by a mob of several hundred men, incited by newspaper articles like the one which urged people to "go Tuesday morning . . . to look at the black and white bretheren and sisters fraternizing, slobbering over each other . . . blaspheming and cursing the constitution of our glorious Union . . ."

At one gathering on rights for women a clergyman seized William Lloyd Garrison by the nose and pulled it hard. True to his nonviolent principles, Garrison said, "Do you feel better, my friend? Do you hope thus to break the force of my argument?"

Many ministers were opposed to women's rights,

claiming that it was God's will for the female to be
subservient to the male. Ernestine was a favorite target
for them, as she was, one clergyman wrote, "a *female*, born of Jewish parents in Poland." That was
sin enough. Besides, she made no effort to hide her
anti-religious views.

Once an entire town became engaged in controversy
over Ernestine Rose. In the fall of 1855 she had been
invited to deliver an anti-slavery lecture in Bangor,
Maine. In advance, a local newspaper had accused her
of being "a female atheist . . . a thousand times below
a prostitute." She replied in a letter to a competing
paper, sparking a feud. By the time she stepped off the
train her name was so well known in the town that
the hall in which she spoke was filled as never before.
She lectured twice, to enthusiastic applause, and was
then invited to neighboring communities. A local editorial commented on the event:

"Mrs. Ernestine L. Rose, whose coming here was
sought to be prevented by . . . forebodings of disaster
and moral ruin, arrived in this city on Monday week,
delivered two lectures . . . and has departed, leaving
the city safe! . . . Mrs. Rose appeared very much like
other women. She is of medium size, dresses 'neat but
not gaudy' . . . is graceful in manner and a rather
effective speaker. . . . Her marked foreign dialect is
the only thing that detracts from an agreeable elocu-
tion . . ."

For some, her foreign accent was objectionable;
others were charmed by it. At one convention, she
was introduced this way: "She was the morning glory
of Poland, the lily of England, and she *is* the rose of
America!" "Her eloquence is irresistible!" one admirer
said.

So irresistible that one day a woman from the audience appeared beside the speaker's platform, placed a baby in Ernestine's arms, and said, "Will you please give her a name?"

Ernestine gazed a while at the baby, said a few words about the responsibility of parents and society towards children, then asked the mother for her last name. The woman told her.

"Then I name her Ernestine Frances Lyons," Ernestine said, gently handing the infant to the mother. Frances was for her deceased friend Frances Wright, another pioneer fighter for woman's rights. The audience burst into applause.

That took place during 1855, which was the busiest year of her life, the year during which she was most in demand as a speaker and traveled the most. She lectured all over New England and the East Coast, went on a two months' tour of Michigan and Ohio, then back again to the Northeast and New York. By year's end, she was utterly exhausted, spent, and sick.

There had been intimations of poor health in various of her letters asking for postponements of engagements. On the way to Kentucky some years before, she had caught a malarial fever and had spent months fighting off fevers and chills. She had tried to get away for a rest, but somehow wherever she went, she could not resist the lure of controversy. Even in South Carolina, where she had sought to rest in a warm climate, she had expressed her hatred of slavery so bluntly that she had to leave town under threat of being feathered and tarred!

By the end of 1855 she knew that if she was to continue to be useful she had to have an extended rest from lectures, meetings, and conventions. She discussed it with her husband, and they decided that a trip to Europe was what she really needed, what they both needed.

During their twenty years of married life, Ernestine had spent months at a time away from home. William Rose was proud of his wife and her achievements; it was his work that enabled her to travel and lecture for causes that were equally dear to him. In her absence, he read and clipped every item about her activities; as his scrapbook grew, so did their days away from one another. The thought of several months together, far from obligations and work, filled them with pleasure.

On May 5, 1856, they stood side by side at the railing of the ship *Northumberland*, remembering the first time they had seen the skyline of New York. They were young then, filled with bright dreams for their new life together, and plans to fight, as Ernestine used to say, "man's glorious battle of freedom." In their mid-forties, they knew only too well how much remained undone. And yet there had been progress; "the world does go forward," Ernestine would say.

They were in Europe for six months, sightseeing in several countries, visiting with their friend and teacher Robert Owen, stopping at a number of spas so Ernestine could rest and regain strength. They tried to go to Poland, "my own poor native land," but were denied admission.

For six months Ernestine stayed away from controversy and from the platform. Within a few days of their return to New York she was involved in a nationwide Women's Rights Convention. It was the seventh such gathering, and it opened on an optimistic note. "Never before has any reform movement gained so much in so short a time," said Lucy Stone, the assembly's president. Indeed, public opinion had come a long way since the first tentative meeting at Seneca Falls; most states had begun to modify their laws governing women, and even men were starting to join the growing movement.

Ernestine Rose made the closing address at the 1856 convention, speaking of woman's role in the upbringing of her children.

"The wisest of all ages have acknowledged," she said to an attentive audience, "that the most important period in human education is in childhood. . . . This most important part of education is left entirely in the hands of the mother. She prepares the soil for future culture. . . . But the mother cannot give what she does not possess; weakness cannot impart strength. With an imperfect education . . . can she develop the powers, call out the energies, and impart a spirit of independence in her sons? . . . The mother must possess these high and noble qualities, or she never can impart them to her offspring."

It was late in the day, and the delegates may have been tired of speeches, but they listened to Ernestine Rose with rapt attention, and applauded her warmly; like so much of her thinking, the words are just as true today as they were then.

The years that followed Ernestine's journey to Europe saw both of her crusades making progress. In 1860 New York State passed a law that granted women nearly everything they had petitioned for—except the vote. It recognized the right of a married woman to be sole owner of any property she had inherited prior to or during marriage; women could make investments, sign contracts; in courts of law, they could sue and be sued. At long last, woman achieved equal control over her children. It was indeed a major victory for the movement.

Prominent men were starting to speak out for women's suffrage, led by Henry Ward Beecher, the most influential minister of the day, and George William Curtis, future editor of *Harper's Weekly;* wealthy supporters began to make contributions to the cause, so that at last the movement was in the black. Among members of the press, the law and even the clergy, some were pressing for better education for women. Yet as the base of support gradually broadened, many new converts were reluctant to be associated with "radical thinkers" like Ernestine Rose, and tried to convince the other women leaders to give her up. Her friends and colleagues of more than twenty years had no intention of heeding such advice.

In May 1860, when Ernestine ascended the platform at the movement's tenth national convention in New York City, she received the kind of applause that is reserved for veterans of many battles. She was fifty years old at that time; streaks of gray were beginning to show in her dark, curly hair. She had had much trouble with her health—rheumatic pains had plagued her for several years—but that day, as she looked out over an audience of two thousand, many of them not even born when she began crusading, she felt boundless optimism. She was at her very best that evening, the Queen of the Platform at the top of her form.

She spoke of her first months in the United States, when she had collected five signatures in five months; that episode had become a legend in the movement.

And then she spoke of the future, when women would finally have the vote and run for elective office.

"She [a woman] could do in Congress, too. Go there and see how your representatives occupy their time, with their feet on the top of their desks, a paper before them, and a thing that ought to be exiled from civilized life [spittoon] at their side, but which must be there if the floor is to be kept clean!"

After the laughter and applause died down, someone in the hall recognized Judge Erastus D. Culver of Brooklyn sitting in the audience. The judge was asked to speak, and what he said thrilled the women who had fought so hard and worked so long. He told them that on that very day several cases had come before his court in which he had been able to invoke for the first time the new law to the advantage of the woman in the case. While the audience stood cheering, Judge Culver continued:

"Now, ladies and gentlemen, I have never been identified with this women's rights movement, but . . . we have got to admit that these indefatigable laborers . . . have at last set the undercurrent in motion. The statute book is their vindication tonight."

Moved by the judge's words, Ernestine rose to thank him for his generous endorsement. Then, recalling the embattled years behind them, she continued, "Freedom, my friends, does not come from the clouds, like a meteor; it does not bloom in one night; it does not come without great efforts and great sacrifices; all who love liberty have to labor for it."

How much longer women would truly have to labor for their freedom they did not know on that May day in 1860. The coming months saw ever more savage conflict between the proponents of slavery and freedom. Most abolitionists had worked for the election of Abraham Lincoln to the presidency, because his views seemed more advanced than those of his opponent. Yet in their eyes he did not go far enough. They wanted total emancipation for all slaves everywhere in the United States. If that meant the secession of the South, so be it; man's freedom should not be compromised in any way.

William Lloyd Garrison, Lucretia Mott, Elizabeth Cady Stanton, Frederick Douglass, himself a former slave, Susan B. Anthony, and Ernestine Rose organized anti-slavery meetings in all the larger cities. They were called "infidels, pestiferous fanatics"; their lives were threatened; everywhere they were met by angry mobs. In Albany they held their meeting only because the mayor, although opposed to their views, vouched for their safety. He took a seat on the platform, placed a revolver on his knee, then, nodding to the evening's chairman, said, "Miss Anthony, you may proceed."

Within a few months, civil war engulfed the nation. For Ernestine and her friends, the principal issue then became the preservation of the Union, and on what terms; the cause of women's rights seemed secondary even to some of its most ardent supporters.

The women did all they could during the conflict to lessen human suffering. They nursed the sick and wounded, knitted socks and scarves, worked the fields while the men were away. In the meantime, New York State's legislators quietly changed the law they had passed, nullifying, at least for a time, many hard-fought advances for women. There was disappointment and bitterness at the setback. Still, while the war raged on, the women felt it was more vital to support the Administration, to strengthen America's resolve to free all slaves.

In the midst of her abolitionist activities, Ernestine Rose could not close her eyes to an attack on the Jewish people. In the pages of the Boston *Investigator* she read an editorial by her friend Horace Seaver in which he slandered all Jews, ancient and modern. She knew that her adopted country was not free of anti-Semitism, but to find it in her favorite progressive journal made her angry.

She wrote Seaver a long, spirited letter, a moving defense of her own people which surprised those who thought that she had cut her ties to Judaism. The editor published her letter, with some comments. Ernestine replied. He wrote again. The debate continued for ten weeks; the more Seaver argued his point, the more he revealed his prejudice. Readers got into the battle, too. A Mr. Woods wrote that he so admired Mrs. Rose "that some years hence I named my only daughter Ernestine Rose Woods."

The battle Ernestine fought in writing in defense of her own people was soon followed by another, still more painful, fought in the ranks of the women's rights movement.

After four years of fighting, the War Between the States had at last come to a close; with war's end, came the, end of slavery as an institution. Ernestine Rose and her abolitionist friends rejoiced that this longed-for day had come to pass. They knew, however, that without the right to vote, freedom was incomplete. An amendment to the Constitution proclaiming universal suffrage, regardless of both color and sex, was their next immediate concern.

When women's help was needed in support of Lincoln's anti-slavery policies, they had been led to believe that suffrage would be theirs at war's end. Now the Administration argued that it could not grant the vote to both Negroes and women right away. This was the Negro's hour, it was said. Women would have to wait a while longer.

The fifteenth constitutional amendment, proclaimed in 1870, extended the right to vote to all *male* citizens regardless of race, color, or "previous condition of servitude." The women were bitter, disappointed, torn. As abolitionists they rejoiced, but as women they felt betrayed. Some actually opposed the amendment. A deep rift developed among the leaders, a group which had held together for three decades against all opposition and had accomplished much. Just when unity was most desperately needed, the movement split; two separate organizations were formed, with the same ultimate aim. It would be several decades before the rift was healed, several more before the vote was ultimately theirs.

As for Ernestine Rose, her days as active crusader were gradually coming to a close. For many years her health had been declining. Severe neuralgia and rheumatic pains made her almost an invalid; only with great difficulty had she risen to speak at one last divisive, stormy meeting in May 1869. Her doctor warned that she needed a complete rest; she sailed for Europe a few weeks later, on June 8.

Once again, wife and husband gazed back at New

York harbor as their ship steamed slowly away. There had been a moving farewell party organized by their faithful friend Susan B. Anthony. They had received thoughtful gifts, including a substantial sum of money collected from colleagues and admirers. It was a welcome present: thirty years of lecturing and travel without charging a fee had left the Roses in reduced circumstances, and they were touched that their friends thought to help. There had been gratifying tributes in the press. "She has long been the best female lecturer in the United States," one paper wrote. Other articles said that she had been Queen of the Platform for over thirty years. Now she was almost sixty and quite ill. Surely she knew, as she watched the shore of the United States fade in the distance, that her active days were now behind her.

She visited several European spas, seeking relief for her pains; rested a lot, spent quiet times with William. She could not tolerate the life of an aging invalid for long, and every so often, when she could, she would accept an invitation to lecture. She longed for the United States. Letters to friends and to the Boston *Investigator* speak of homesickness and of her yearning to return to the heart of the struggle. Yet her health would not permit much activity, and financial considerations made it more practical for them to stay in England than to return to New York.

In 1882 William Rose died. Ernestine never fully recovered from her grief. They had been devoted to each other, had shared hopes and ideals, struggles and victories. After his death, Ernestine seldom left her home. Sitting in her London flat, usually alone, she kept in touch with the world she once knew through

newspapers or letters to her friend Susan B. Anthony
and a few others. Even writing was difficult; illness
made her hands tremble. Yet she followed news of the
women's rights movement, glad that the rift between
the two factions appeared healed and that new young
leaders were emerging from the ranks, confident that
in time the vote would be theirs. "Go on, go on! Halt
not and rest not," she wrote to a convention of the
National Woman's Suffrage Association.

She died in Brighton on August 4, 1892, and was
buried beside her husband, as she had wished. She had
long been ready for her life to end, "if I may call my
present inaction life, which I don't," she had written,
"for action only is life." "But I have lived," she would
say thoughtfully to friends, "I have lived."

"Let Our Minds Be Bold"

Louis D. Brandeis

1856–1941

Louis D. Brandeis, 1856–1941.

LOOKING BACK ON HIS CHILDHOOD, late in life, Justice Louis D. Brandeis still remembered the turmoil that Civil War brought to his native city of Louisville, Kentucky.

"I remember helping my mother carry out food and coffee to the men from the North," he recalled. "The streets seemed full of them always. But there were times when the rebels came so near that we could hear the firing. At one such time my father moved us across the river. Those were my first memories."

Across the Ohio River from Louisville was Indiana, a state loyal to the Union; south of Kentucky was Tennessee, a secessionist state. Kentucky had declared itself neutral, but among its people were intense partisans of both sides. A family like the Brandeises, who were openly anti-slavery and pro-Union, had good reason to be concerned about reprisals.

Adolph and Frederika Brandeis were opposed to slavery in any form: they knew from experience the bitter taste of prejudice and oppression. They had come to the United States from Central Europe, from the beautiful old city of Prague, after the failure of the rebellions that swept through the continent in 1848. The repression that followed and a pervasive lack of opportunity, drove millions of German-speaking men and women toward the New World during the 1840s, 1850s, and 1860s. They were rich and poor, farmers and intellectuals, Catholics, Protestants, and Jews. Those among them who were of Jewish background, like the Brandeises, left behind centuries of insecurity and ill-treatment.

Adolph Brandeis, his fiancee, Frederika Dembitz, and their families—twenty-six people in all, with twenty-seven great chests filled with belongings—landed in New York City in 1849. By barge, steamboat, and train, they made their way to the Ohio River valley, lived for a time in Cincinnati, then in Madison, Indiana. By the time Louis David Brandeis was born, on November 13, 1856, his father was well established as a grain and produce merchant in the riverfront city of Louisville, Kentucky.

Louis was the youngest of four children; Father and Mother Brandeis made sure their sons and daughters were exposed to every advantage the new country had to offer: good books and music, a fine education, and most especially the freedom to explore new ideas and to exchange them freely with one another. The Brandeis dinner table was the setting for many lively discussions in English and German; friends and family often joined them for the noon or evening meal.

Louis' favorite was Uncle Lewis Dembitz, his mother's younger brother. He was a lawyer, with a broad view of the law's influence on human lives and with interests that ranged from astronomy to the Bible and Jewish history. As young Louis grew up, it seemed to him that his uncle knew everything there was to know in life, and he determined to follow in his footsteps. So deep was Lewis Dembitz's influence on his nephew that in his honor the young man changed his middle name from David to Dembitz.

All the Brandeis children were good students, but it was evident from the very start that Louis had the makings of an outstanding scholar. With his brother Alfred, he attended the German and English Academy, where the two languages were taught on a par; by the time Louis was in his teens and Papa announced that the family was going on an extended trip to Europe, it seemed quite natural for Louis to decide to attend school in Germany for a time.

The stay in Europe was not entirely for pleasure. The economic picture was poor in the United States in 1872, and the elder Brandeis worried that a depression might be on the way. Rather than wait for a crash to wipe them out, he decided to close down his business and spend some months away. Louis was sixteen then; Alfred, his brother and best friend, eighteen; Amy and Fannie were twenty and twenty-one. The journey was filled with meaning for them all: for the parents, a return to their birthplace, for the four young people, a chance to visit the great cities of Europe, to see the places where their parents grew up.

Louis enrolled in a boarding school in Dresden, Germany. Even in a foreign country, in a school with strict discipline and rigid academic requirements, his gifts of scholarship shone through. His teachers and fellow students learned to admire the tall young man with black hair and deep blue eyes, who spoke German almost as well as they did. He, in turn, responded to the demanding schedule of courses with enthusiasm. "In Dresden, I learned how to think," he was to say years later. His grades were excellent, and he enjoyed the work, but after a time the strict rules began to pall.

One evening Louis had been out visiting friends and on returning to his dormitory found he had forgotten his key. It was late; the entrance door was locked. He walked around the long stone building until he stood

just below his own room. He looked up to his win-
dow and whistled sharply, until his roommate heard
him and opened the front door. Whistling, it then
turned out, was strictly against the rules, a habit most
unsuitable for young gentlemen of good family. For
his rude behavior, Louis was given a severe reprimand
and warned not to whistle again.

For quite some time Louis had been dreaming of the
freedom he had enjoyed at home in America, of long
rides in the open country, walks along the Ohio River,
the ability to decide for himself. In Kentucky it was
all right to whistle! Suddenly he was ready to go
home and continue his studies there.

He knew by then that law would be his field; he
also knew where he wanted to study, if at all possible.
From American friends in Dresden he had heard about
Harvard University; when he landed in the United
States in May 1875, he went directly to Cambridge,
Massachusetts, to apply for admission to the Harvard
Law School. He was accepted and entered in the fall.

It seemed to him as he walked by the green lawns
and red brick buildings of Harvard, as he strolled
along the Charles River and considered New England's
influence on American thinking, that here was where
he wanted to continue his education, here was where
he wanted to live. There was never a time when he
regretted his decision. He missed his family while he
attended law school and wrote them frequent, affec-
tionate letters; to his brother he wrote almost every
day, even if only a brief sentence or two. But Harvard, and later Boston, and New England, claimed his
loyalty for the rest of his life.

When he entered Harvard in the fall of 1875 he

had $200 borrowed from Alfred. Their father was in no position to pay for his law school education; on returning from Europe the elder Brandeis had had to start in business all over again. But Alfred had been working for two years and was glad to help his younger brother at the start. Once in Harvard, Louis was sure that he would find a way to earn enough to put himself through law school.

"Mr. Brandeis had hardly taken his seat in our classroom before his remarkable talents were discovered," wrote one of his classmates some years later. And it was true that the tall, slender eighteen-year-old, youngest in the class, became outstanding almost right away. Other students came to him for help in their studies; without seeming effort, he was able to earn enough as a tutor to pay his bills and repay his brother's loan.

He enjoyed classes, read endlessly from textbooks, and could barely contain his enthusiasm for Harvard's well-stocked library. For each law club meeting he prepared as if it were the most important court case of his career. He read and searched, dug out new evidence, came up with original approaches. "The law has her grip on me, and I suppose I cannot escape her clutches," he wrote home.

One frightening note crept into that first year at law school. Toward spring of 1876 his eyes started to hurt; often they were tired and bloodshot, sometimes his vision blurred. The flickering flames of gas lamps caused frequent eye strain among those who studied as intensely as he. Friends told him to ease off, but he would not.

During the summer, back at his parents' home, Louis

consulted several physicians; they all said that the condition was serious, that he might go blind, and advised
that he give up studying law. That was unthinkable!
Louis Brandeis could no more do that than stop breath-
ing! He tried one more doctor, a well-known spe-
cialist in New York, who examined him, considered
his chosen field, and remarked, "It won't hurt you to
read less and think more."

Back at Harvard the young man tried to think of
how to follow this advice and yet absorb the information he needed. He found that several of his classmates
were willing to read assignments out loud to him; one
of them was Samuel D. Warren, Jr., who became his
lifelong friend and first law partner. Louis would sit
in his room with his eyes closed, concentrating all his
attention on what was being read; he found it invalu-
able training, for it sharpened his memory and taught
him to store legal knowledge in his mind.

By the second and final year Louis Brandeis had
achieved such high grades that he was chosen valedic-
torian of his class. Then a problem arose: he was only
twenty, and Harvard had a rule that to graduate from
law school you had to be twenty-one. At the very last
moment, on commencement morning, the trustees sus-
pended the regulation, and he was allowed to take his
place with the graduating class.

The following fall found him back on campus for a
year of graduate work; part-time jobs as a tutor and
proctor enabled him to meet expenses. "Those years
were among the happiest of my life," he told a friend.
"I worked! For me the world's center was Cambridge."

Yet in the fall of 1878, when he was ready for his

first job in the law, Boston did not appear to be the
best place to start. The most promising offer came
from St. Louis, Missouri, through the auspices of his
brother-in-law Charles Nagel; there was a room waiting for him at Fannie's and Charles's home and a job
as law clerk at $50 a month, a good salary at the time
From the outset he was not happy in St. Louis. The
city was hot and humid, he had few friends, and he
found the work dull. He missed New England! A few
months later came a letter from Sam Warren, lifting
his spirits: his friend suggested that he come back to
Boston and form a partnership with him. Brandeis sent
off a telegram right away: SHALL WRITE FULLY TO-
NIGHT. IT SEEMS A GOOD THING.

A good thing it was, for both young men; they
were highly intelligent and ambitious, both fascinated
with the law, well suited as partners. Warren, through
his family's high-placed friends in Boston, brought in
the first clients, but Louis Brandeis had achieved quite
a reputation while at Harvard, and he, too, had good
contacts.

From the beginning Brandeis was sure he had made
the right decision. Every once in a while he would
feel a touch of longing for his family so far away, but
even then his enthusiasm for Boston soon won out.
Each day would start with a long walk after breakfast,
then he would spend the morning as law clerk to
Chief Justice Horace Gray of the Supreme Judicial
Court of Massachusetts. For two years the salary he
received from the judge took care of his needs, until
the firm of Warren & Brandeis, Counselors at Law,
began to prosper. After lunch Brandeis would work
with Sam Warren on their business until dinner time.

"The evenings of last week I spent as follows," he wrote his mother soon after the start of their firm. He described a trip to the laundry, an evening sail, a visit to the Warrens' lakeside home. "This is, indeed, an immense advantage of Boston," he commented. "One can enjoy living, and nature is so beautiful . . . oh, how beautiful are heaven and earth here, hills and water, nature and art!"

The two young partners did not become rich overnight, but they had a way of winning cases, first small ones, then gradually more important ones. Many of their first clients were Harvard friends, many were people active in public life. Through them Brandeis became interested in Boston politics, in social services, in the budding labor movement. Everything he learned he brought to bear on his work in the law; from the very start his success as a lawyer often rested on his amazing memory, on the pertinent facts he was able to call on at a moment's thought. Frequently he knew more about the business of his opponents than they did. He moved around a courtroom with one hand in his pocket, quiet, gentle, but devastatingly thorough.

He loved the challenge of trial work, of new cases, of the varied problems he was asked to solve. When Harvard Law School offered him an assistant professorship in law, he thought it over with his usual care, but then declined. He wanted above all things to be independent, financially secure, free of having to work for money. One of his most dearly held beliefs was that a man must spend less than he earns in order to achieve this freedom. To this end, he was thrifty in everything he did. The rooms he rented, the furnishings in his office, the food he ate, all were as plain

as he could find them. He was frugal with his own
time as well, making each hour of the day count as
much as possible. Nobody was ever kept waiting in his
office; he was brief and direct in all his business
dealings, to the point that some found him abrupt and
cold. Yet he had a gift for close friendships and knew
full well the need for relaxation. His experience at
Harvard had taught him that he must not allow himself to overwork. He would go horseback riding with
Sam Warren, canoeing or sailing with other friends,
spend weekends at the seashore home of Oliver Wendell Holmes, Jr., who would become one of the country's foremost jurists, and Brandeis' ally on the Supreme
Court.

Through his friends Jack and Mary O'Sullivan, he
became interested in the labor movement; through
clients, he learned about the world of large corporations. Gradually Louis Brandeis began to see the need
for change in our society, the necessity for men and
women to work toward reform. After some years of
building up the business of Warren & Brandeis, he
began to have a little time to serve on civic committees and even sometimes handle a case without fee, if
he felt the cause needed defending. By the time he
was thirty-three years old, in 1890, he was considered
one of the finest legal men in the New England
region. That year was to bring great changes in his
life.

In March of 1890 Louis Brandeis was suddenly sum-
moned home by the tragic news that his sister Fannie
had died. She was only thirty-nine years old, and they
had been very close to one another; Louis was crushed
by the untimely loss. In Louisville he did his best to

comfort his parents and the rest of the family. He spent many hours visiting with his sister Amy and her husband, his brother Alfred, his uncles and aunts. It was while visiting one of his uncles that he met the young woman who would share his life.

Alice Goldmark was Louis' second cousin from New York; they had met once before, when she was six. Now she was twenty-four, slim and attractive, with large brown eyes and a low, pleasant voice. Alice was shy, but when Louis drew her out he found they had many interests in common. He eagerly accepted her invitation to visit the Goldmark home; as soon as he went back to Boston he began to make weekend trips to New York and that summer, he spent several weeks at the Goldmarks' country home.

Almost from the start, Alice and Louis knew they were in love; that summer Alice confided to her diary, "His eyes are always upon me . . . we have found each other."

They were married the following March and moved into a slim red brick house on Beacon Hill, within easy walk of Brandeis' office. It was a small house, three windows wide, three stories and an attic high, and plainly furnished. Louis Brandeis had not forgotten his pledge to himself: a man must set aside part of his earnings to achieve freedom. His bride agreed whole-heartedly. Their lives as well as their furnishings would be plain and simple, and efficient, so that Louis' time and mental energies could be devoted to things that were important to them both.

By 1891, Louis Brandeis was in sole charge of the law firm. Sam Warren had taken over the management of his family's holdings on his father's death, and although the firm's name remained unchanged, the two men had dissolved their partnership. They remained friends; they would still meet and have long talks on legal problems. Out of their mutual concern came an article in the *Harvard Law Review* on the right to privacy; it contained principles that had never been set forth before. It was said at the time that Sam Warren and Louis Brandeis had added a new chapter to American law.

There was much in Brandeis' attitude on the law that was original. He believed not only in knowing all the legislation and facts concerning a particular case, but in being familiar with the business of his client and of the other parties involved. He was one of the first lawyers in the country who acted as an adviser to his clients, not merely as advocate; his business judgment and advice were highly valued and made him one of the most successful commercial lawyers of his time.

In the 1890s it was business law that was Brandeis' most important area of work. Preparing a series of university lectures on the subject, reading newspapers and reports from various areas of the United States, he became more and more aware of the unrest and discontent among workers in businesses throughout the nation. In factories, mines, and railroad crews, people were working long, arduous hours under unhealthy and often dangerous conditions, and the pay they brought home was barely enough to keep their families alive. The movement to organize these workers into unions that could protect their rights was just beginning to get under way; for the most part, employers looked upon unions as the enemy, believing it was their God-given right to run their business as only they saw fit.

While Louis Brandeis was researching material for some lectures he was to deliver at the Massachusetts Institute of Technology, in July 1892, a brutal strike in Homestead, Pennsylvania, sent waves of shock across the land. Armed strikebreakers had been hired to prevent a walkout by some steel workers who were protesting a wage cut. Shots were fired. Many men on both sides were wounded in the battle, some were killed. Saddened and dismayed, Louis Brandeis threw away the notes he had prepared, and began to look at the entire picture in a different way.

"It took the shock of that battle," he said later, "to turn my mind definitely toward a searching study of the relations of labor to industry."

It was a turning point in his career. From that time on, he was sure that present laws were inadequate for dealing with the complex relations in the modern factory system. He worked to improve the ethics of the business world with better legislation and to protect the workers. Because of his superb understanding of business, many of his clients, executives of large corporations, listened to his advice. Not all of them, to be sure. His insistence that a client had to be right before he would accept a case, his low tolerance for less competent men, his brisk efficiency, made many people hate him. This caused him no concern. He had as many clients as he wished; his fees kept growing. By following his own beliefs and investing a substantial part of his earnings, he became wealthy. By the time he was forty he was free, as he had planned to be,

able to take on causes that he thought worthwhile
without regard to payment.

He felt strongly that most lawyers of his day were
identified too much with large corporations, that they
had lost sight of their opportunity "to protect *also* the
interests of the people." He meant to spend a good
part of his time attempting to correct social problems.

During the 1890s he fought against lobby groups
that tried to bribe legislators; he became involved in a
movement to humanize institutions for the poor; he
fought against a powerful company that tried to control Boston's transportation system. He drew a clear
line of distinction between work for a private client
and efforts on behalf of a public cause. From corporations and wealthy individuals he received fees that
were in line with his reputation as a famous attorney.
For what he considered public service, he would accept no payment.

This was a most unusual practice in his day and
caused much comment and a good deal of suspicion of
his motives. What was behind Brandeis' efforts against
railroad companies, people wondered? If he wished to
aid a certain cause, asked reporters, why not contribute
money to it, instead of offering his services as lawyer?
The answer he gave on one occasion sheds light on his
character, and his reasons.

"Some men buy diamonds and rare works of art,"
he explained. "My luxury is to invest my surplus effort, beyond what is required for the proper support
of my family, to the pleasure of taking up a problem
. . . and helping to solve it for the people without
receiving any compensation . . . I have only one life,

and it is short enough," he continued, "why waste it on things I don't want most? I don't want money or property most—I want to be free."

He knew that as he gave less time to his firm's work and more to public causes, the income of his partners and employees might decrease, so he repaid the firm for time he spent for public work.

In all this, he had complete support from Alice, who shared his lack of interest in possessions. And although he did not indulge his family in the luxuries that many men of his standing took for granted, he was always generous with his affection and time. Home and family formed a vital part of his life.

From the time his two daughters were infants— Susan was born in 1893, Elizabeth, three years later— father and daughters always started out the day together. As they grew into childhood, breakfast was a time for conversation and books; everyone would take turns at reading sections of favorite stories. He was intensely interested in the children's education, even giving them his own version of early legal training: when they were eight and five respectively, the girls signed a contract agreeing to clean and shine their father's shoes six days a week for five cents each, and they lived up to it! Louis Brandeis always walked to work; Susan and Elizabeth would walk beside him, in their starched dresses and high button shoes, down Beacon Hill, then continue on to school, while their father went to his office. They lived near the Charles River, so Brandeis taught his wife and daughters to canoe; in winter, they were avid ice-skaters.

Each year the entire month of August was devoted to rest and relaxation. The family would rent a cottage on Cape Cod, where the famous attorney spent his days teaching his young daughters how to swim, collecting shells, exploring inlets and streams in a canoe, reading a great variety of books and periodicals.

September 1 he would return to Boston well refreshed, ready to take on the next case, fight the next battle. In or out of the courtroom, he made outstanding contributions to the progress of social reform during the early years of the twentieth century. In each crusade, he would try to do more than right a wrong; he insisted on creating new conditions, new agencies for the public benefit; he attempted to educate the public to the problem, so it would not recur. During these years he took on the giants of the life insurance companies, fighting for the right of working people to be provided with reliable and inexpensive insurance; he fought against the monopolistic policies of the New Haven Railroad in a battle that continued for nine years.

In 1907, a banner year in his career, he was asked to defend an Oregon state law establishing a ten-hour work day as a maximum for women. For years social reform groups had been working to get laws passed by various states limiting the hours men and women could work and setting up standards for their safety. Employers fought bitterly against such laws, insisting that they alone should set the rules. The Oregon law was being challenged in the United States Supreme Court; if it was overthrown, all past accomplishments would be lost.

Brandeis agreed to represent the state of Oregon; he appeared before the nine black-robed justices with an argument in favor of the law which was so new and unconventional that it made legal history. Until that time, most legal briefs had quoted past decisions to make their point. The "Brandeis Brief"—the term became famous after that—dealt with the human condition. In more than one hundred pages, Brandeis quoted evidence drawn from reports of factory inspectors, nurses, and doctors on the effects of long hours on the workers' health and on the inferior output this produced. He meant to acquaint the highest tribunal in the land with the realities of modern industrial life. His method worked: the Court unanimously upheld the Oregon law. As a result, other states began to set standards for hours, wages, safety, and health of their workers.

The daily rights, the daily needs of working people soon became Brandeis' overriding concern. In 1910 he found himself mediating a garment workers' strike in New York City. Some 50,000 sewing-machine operators, cutters, and pressers had walked out on their employers on New York's Lower East Side. Their bosses were not the industrial giants involved in most labor disputes; they were mostly small operators, enterprising men with a few hundred dollars' capital and a dozen sewing machines, who set up shop in a tenement house and hired recent immigrants with few choices of employment.

Louis D. Brandeis had never before set foot on the Lower East Side. In the nation's greatest city was an area as crowded and unhealthy as any factory town, as any ghetto in Europe. Entire families lived in single dark, airless rooms, and often worked there, too, men and women bent over a pressing iron or a sewing machine for ten, twelve hours a day, yet not earning enough to feed their families.

Most of the striking workers had recently arrived from Eastern Europe, Jews from Russia and Poland, Hungary and Romania, seeking refuge from unbearable conditions and persecutions in their native lands. Yet these men and women, totally dependent on the meager wages they earned, were brave enough to take their place on the picket line, to risk unemployment and hunger for the sake of some small improvement in their lives. They had taken a long, dangerous journey drawn by a vision of what America could be. Looking into their world, Louis D. Brandeis was touched and inspired, determined to help them find a way.

Negotiations dragged on for weeks, in the heat of New York City's summer. Ten representatives of the employers sat on one side of a long table, ten workers faced them. Brandeis chaired the meetings, pleading, warning, asking each side to listen to the other. As grievances were examined one by one, his creative mind designed new possibilities. Early in September a "protocol of peace" was announced, and the strikers, idle for three months, became a cheering, celebrating crowd.

Louis D. Brandeis had brought the workers in the clothing trade collective bargaining: the right to negotiate their own wages and hours with their employers. In turn, the workers caused important changes in his thinking. For the first time in his life, he had come in contact with a large group of Jewish people. These impoverished immigrants from Eastern Europe were different from his own cultured, middle-class Jewish family; their customs and the Yiddish language they spoke were alien to him. Yet he felt a strong bond with them. He admired their high intelligence and zeal, their vision of democracy and their talent for negotiation and self-government. He began to think of them as "his people"; the journey to New York's Lower East Side had turned into a deeply felt experience.

When he returned to his practice in Boston he felt a need to learn more about Jewish history and culture; though his family was Jewish on both sides, they had never attended synagogue nor had any formal training in religion. He began to read about the young Zionist movement, the dream of a small band of idealists in Europe to found a Jewish homeland, a country to which all Jews could freely go. His interest in Zionism, sparked by his involvement with the New York City garment workers in 1910, received new impetus two years later from a different source. In more than one way, 1912 was a watershed year for Louis Brandeis.

In 1912 Brandeis was fifty-six years old. He was successful as a corporation lawyer; at the same time he had a reputation as a reformer and crusader. Although he was well aware of the ties between business, labor, and the political process, up to that time he had never been involved in party politics, preferring a nonpartisan position. In 1912 he received a call from Woodrow Wilson, the governor of New Jersey, who was preparing to run for the presidency of the United States on the Democratic ticket.

The two men were similar in many ways, in appearance and character. Both were tall and slender, both wore glasses, were proper and correct in dress and manner. Both were reserved—cold, some people said—both were southern-born. They could be blunt and direct and earn resentment as well as admiration. Wilson shared Brandeis' fear of big enterprise, believing that economic domination could lead to political control; like many reformers, he had not been able to devise a program for overcoming the "curse of bigness." Brandeis helped the future President shape a program which they named the "New Freedom." It called for regulating competition and creating a federal trade commission to supervise business practices. All through the fall of 1912 Brandeis campaigned actively for Wilson; among many progressives, who were torn between voting for Wilson or voting for "Teddy" Roosevelt, the Progressive party candidate, Brandeis' support was the deciding factor.

After Wilson's election there was much speculation about a Cabinet appointment for Brandeis. Would he be named Secretary of Commerce or of Labor? Or perhaps Attorney General? Reporters asked Louis Brandeis what he thought.

"Don't believe all you hear," he would reply. He thought there might be opposition to his receiving a Cabinet appointment. He knew he had made many enemies in the course of his crusades; his fondness for "knocking heads right and left," as he liked to say, had angered powerful people. So had his righteous stance. Yet he did not foresee the avalanche of adverse mail concerning him that descended on the President's desk; he could not have guessed the viciousness of his opponents.

He was accused of having no integrity, no legal ethics, of being a radical and revolutionist. There were objections to his being Jewish; some letters and articles alluded to this in veiled terms, others openly distrusted "the workings of the Jewish mind." It grew into a smear campaign. Wilson, who had won the Democratic nomination by a slim margin, felt he could not antagonize any section of his party. He wanted Brandeis in his Cabinet. He needed "men who are brave. Men who are efficient. Men who have imagination," he said. But he bowed to the pressure.

Despite the inevitable disappointment and hurt, Brandeis never withheld his counsel from the President. Over the next few years he traveled frequently from Boston to Washington, testifying before congressional committees, defending controversial laws before the Supreme Court, helping Wilson shape his administration. At the same time, he became deeply involved in the Zionist movement.

In the course of the electoral campaign of 1912, Brandeis had befriended Jacob de Haas, editor of the *Jewish Advocate* of Boston. De Haas had previously worked in London with Theodor Herzl, founder of modern Zionism. De Haas spoke to Brandeis at great length about the sufferings of their fellow Jews in Eastern Europe, about the dream of founding a Jewish nation in the land of the Bible, to be settled by those escaping persecution. He described the many people working to bring this dream to life; he told Brandeis that Brandeis' uncle, Lewis Dembitz, had played an important role in the movement prior to his death some years before.

Brandeis had already accepted the ideal of a Jewish nation; de Haas convinced him to take an active part in forming one. During 1913 the prominent attorney appeared in city after city in the United States, speaking to audiences of the need for a Jewish national state, telling them of the struggles and achievements of the pioneers who had already settled in Palestine, some 150,000 by that time. His listeners were rabbis, teachers, businessmen and women, leaders of Jewish groups; this new crusade represented for Brandeis a positive response to the ugly, humiliating exposure to prejudice he had experienced in the previous months. He was frank in admitting his shortcomings:

"I have been to a great extent separated from Jews," he told an audience in 1914. "I am very ignorant in things Jewish. But recent experiences, public and professional, have taught me this: I find Jews possessed of those very qualities which we of the twentieth century seek to develop in our struggle for justice and democracy: a deep moral feeling which makes them capable of noble acts; a deep sense of the brotherhood of man; and a high intelligence, the fruit of three thousand years of civilization.

"These experiences have made me feel that the Jewish people have something which should be saved for the world . . . and that it is our duty to pursue that method of saving which most promises success . . ."

By late summer of 1914, World War I was sweeping across Europe, and those Jews caught in the path of the conflict were exposed to extreme suffering and famine. Relief efforts had to be organized in haste; Brandeis agreed to head the operating committee of the World Zionist Organization whose headquarters had been moved to the United States. With customary energy, he plunged headlong into the work, raising funds and sending shiploads of supplies to Jews trapped in Central Europe and in the Middle East, organizing the movement in this country. "Zionist affairs are really the important things in life now," he wrote his brother in 1915.

Many American Jews, including members of Brandeis' own family, doubted the wisdom of the Zionist idea. To those who wondered if they could be good Americans and good Zionists at the same time, Brandeis replied: "Every American Jew who aids in advancing the Jewish settlement in Palestine, though he feels that neither he nor his descendants will ever live there, will likewise be a better man and a better American for doing so." He saw Zionism as an extension of the American ideal; both, he felt, shared a "deep sense of the brotherhood of man."

From 1914 to 1921 Louis D. Brandeis was the acknowledged leader of American Zionism. During those years, membership in the Zionist Organization of America grew from 12,000 to more than 170,000, spearheading a powerful world force. In 1921 Brandeis unexpectedly resigned as leader, ending a long-simmering dispute between two factions in the organization, which came to a head after the end of the war in 1918. By that time he had reached another milestone in his extraordinary career in public life.

All through the first term of Wilson's administration, Brandeis had been the President's trusted adviser and friend. Many prominent people had been disap-

Attorney and reformer, Louis Brandeis was appointed to the Supreme Court of the United States in 1916.

pointed over Wilson's failure to appoint him to the Cabinet; after his re-election in 1916, the President determined to bring Brandeis officially into the government at the first opportunity. On January 28, 1916, soon after Congress had returned from Christmas recess, the President sent a message to the Senate:

"I nominate Louis D. Brandeis of Massachusetts," the clerk read out to a half-empty chamber, "to be Associate Justice of the Supreme Court of the United States, vice [to replace] Joseph Rucker Lamar, deceased. Signed, Woodrow Wilson. The White House. 28 January 1916."

The senators sat stunned, looking at one another in amazement. They had known that the President was considering various candidates to replace Justice Lamar. Several well-known names had been put forth; many Republicans had suggested former President Taft. But Louis Brandeis to the Supreme Court! And without even consulting party leaders! It was a disgrace!

Reporters left the press gallery and ran to phone their newspapers, and soon headlines across the nation heralded the appointment. Editorials bemoaned the fact that a reformer—a radical, some said—had been appointed to the highest court, the tribunal which most people felt was meant to be the conservator of the country's institutions. The headline in the New York *Sun* was a blunt prophecy: FIRST JEW EVER PICKED FOR BENCH. LONG AND BITTER FIGHT EXPECTED IN THE SENATE OVER CONFIRMATION.

It was, indeed, one of the longest and bitterest fights ever waged in the Senate over a presidential nomination. For almost five months the Senate investigated every aspect of Louis Brandeis' life and qualifications;

by the time it was over, almost everyone in the country had taken sides in the debate.

Before the Judiciary Committee of the Senate came every enemy Brandeis had ever made during his busy and controversial career; representatives of railroad interests and life insurance companies accused him of "breach of faith and unprofessional conduct"; conservative members of the American Bar Association called him "not a fit person to be a member of the Supreme Court of the United States."

To support the nomination, many came forward on Brandeis' behalf: enlightened businessmen and attorneys, labor leaders, social workers, college professors, and writers testified to his character and ability. Witnesses for both sides were carefully questioned and cross-questioned; as the senators investigated each charge, they could uncover no misdeeds at all. It became evident that the opposition was sparked by people who resented Brandeis' personality or by powerful interests who did not want a liberal on the court. Anti-Semitism was repeatedly denied as a motive, but there is no doubt that it did play its part.

When the full Senate at long last voted on June 1, the nomination of Louis D. Brandeis to the Supreme Court was confirmed by a vote of 47 to 22.

That afternoon, when the newspapers announced BRANDEIS CONFIRMED TO SUPREME COURT, his daughter Susan was in New York City, attending a conference on women's right to vote. A lady sitting next to her looked at the headline, then turned and said, with distaste in her voice, "I see they confirmed that Jew Brandeis as a Justice of the Supreme Court."

Susan Brandeis looked at the woman coldly. "You

are certainly speaking to the right person, madam," she replied. "Mr. Brandeis happens to be my father!"

That same day Mrs. Brandeis received a letter from her friend Belle La Follette, wife of Robert M. La Follette, the progressive senator from Wisconsin who had been Brandeis' most steadfast supporter throughout the confirmation fight. "There will be an end to all this wicked business," wrote Mrs. La Follette. "As soon as Louis is a member of the Court his enemies will take to cover. I suppose some of them will be claiming they made him Judge. The fight . . . will end with the oath of office."

Opposition did not die down that quickly, but over the years even those who differed with his ideals admitted that Mr. Justice Brandeis was one of the finest judges ever to have sat on the Court. He served on the Supreme Court for twenty-three years, during the administrations of five different Presidents. For almost the entire time a majority of the justices were conservatives; Brandeis' views were expressed in minority opinions, in which he was often joined by his old friend from Boston days, Oliver Wendell Holmes, Jr.

Justice Holmes was seventy-five years old when Brandeis joined the court, the oldest judge in years but youngest in his thinking. Together, "Holmes and Brandeis dissenting," they wrote historic opinions which upheld the rights of individuals as against property rights and against infringement by the state. Brandeis was passionately convinced that in a free society men and women must be encouraged to differ with each other and with the state. Only by listening to opposing ideas, he argued in his dissents, can one hope to reach the truth. "If we would guide by the light of reason, we must let our minds be bold."

The 1920s and early 1930s saw the conservative majority on the Court declare unconstitutional many attempts by the states to protect working men and women and regulate the power of industrial giants. In his minority opinions Justice Brandeis tried to convince his colleagues, and the country, on the necessity for such legislation and on the need for law to keep up with the times and relate to contemporary life.

The same passion for education and reform that inspired him as an attorney made him a memorable judge. He wrote more than five hundred opinions during his years on the bench; toward the end of his tenure, many of his earlier dissents were being referred to as if they had been majority opinions. His views had taken hold.

During Brandeis' years on the Court, his advice and viewpoint were sought by a great variety of people who seemed to agree with President Wilson that "a talk with Brandeis always sweeps the cobwebs out of one's mind." The Sunday afternoon teas that Justice and Mrs. Brandeis always held were a meeting place for people young and old, students and diplomats, businessmen and politicians, who wished an opportunity of a few moments' conversation with the judge. He especially enjoyed talking with his daughters' young friends; he welcomed their fresh, open point of view, their hopes for the future of mankind.

He was delighted that Susan and Elizabeth had chosen fields related to his own. Both had gone to law school; Elizabeth specialized in labor legislation, an interest which he shared. Susan was practicing law in New York City; on one proud, unprecedented day Mr. Justice Brandeis had to excuse himself from taking part in a decision because his daughter had argued the case before the Court.

Both daughters married and had families. Justice and Mrs. Brandeis often had the pleasure of sharing their Cape Cod cottage with their grandchildren. There, Grandfather Brandeis once more led adventurous walks and treasure hunts on the beach, just as he had when his own children were young.

In time, the walks had to be shorter; as he grew old, the judge knew that he must conserve his energies. With customary efficiency, he would lie down to rest if he felt his mind was getting tired; he still wanted to give every issue at hand his very best.

Even when he was well into his seventies, the areas of his concern reached far and wide. Despite all setbacks, despite the lengthening shadows of a second world war, Brandeis continued to work towards a national home for the Jews, using his influence with important people in the United States and abroad. He was instrumental in getting American approval for the Balfour Declaration, the document by which Great Britain paved the way for Jewish settlement in what was then Palestine. He did not live to see his dream fulfilled. Another decade had to pass, another war, years of unprecedented horror, persecution, and murder, before the State of Israel could emerge. But he was one of those who helped lay the foundations.

By 1938 he knew his strength was running out. He was home ill a good part of the winter; in February of 1939 he sent a letter to President Franklin D. Roosevelt, resigning from the Supreme Court.

"There is nothing I can do but to accede to your retirement," wrote FDR to the man he used to call "prophet Isaiah." He expressed hope "that you will be spared for many long years to render additional services to mankind."

Then came another letter, which sums up Brandeis' life and influence far better than the eulogies of famous men.

"Dearest Father," wrote his daughter Elizabeth. "It is hard for me to write. All the things I want to say sound mawkish—or presumptuous from me to you. I cannot bear to use any words at this time that do not ring true. I hope you know what is in my heart even if I cannot get it said.

"I know that there is no cause for grieving. Everything must have an end. And the life and work that you can look back upon must give you contentment and satisfaction. As for me, my appreciation of what you are and have done keeps increasing as I grow older and better able to understand.

"If the lessons you have taught do not seem to have been learned very well yet, that is not for any lack on your part. Measuring my words, I do not see how any one person could have done more than you have done.

"But of course I do feel sad—regardless. I suppose ends are always sad. Paul and I, along with hundreds, probably thousands, of others, will be trying to carry on different parts of your work and trying to catch something of the spirit in which you have worked. But we shall all know how inadequate we are and how far we fall short of the standards you set. But I know you will be generous in your judgment of us, and at least, despite our other limitations, our love and admiration for you will continue to be just about unlimited! Elizabeth."

Justice Brandeis lived two more years in retirement, frail in health but ever interested in new ideas, in young people, in social reform. He died October 5, 1941, a month before his eighty-fifth birthday. His legacy for us today is all around us: in our system of Social Security; in free legal assistance for the poor and public service law firms; in the movements for consumer protection and conservation; in the growing opposition to wiretaps; in our intense concern for individual liberties and civil rights.

Nurse to the Millions

Lillian D.Wald

1867–1940

Lillian D. Wald, 1867–1940.

THE TWO YOUNG WOMEN walked briskly as they talked, one fashionably dressed in the style of the late 1880s, the other, somewhat older, wearing a uniform and carrying a black bag.

"Here we are. This is my sister's home." Lillian, the dark-haired, younger woman, stopped, and rang the doorbell. The nurse followed her in, talked a few moments with the doctor who met her in the hall, then went into the bedroom to her patient. Lillian Wald stayed back, glad to have a few moments to herself, to catch her breath and sort out the events of the past several hours.

She had been visiting her married sister, Julia Barry, at the sea shore, when Julia suddenly felt ill. A physician was called. He suggested a nurse to care for Julia and asked Lillian if she would call for the nurse and bring her back right away. Concern for her sister had prompted Lillian to ask a million questions as they hurried towards the Barry home. She had seldom been ill in her life; she had never spoken to a trained nurse before, and she was fascinated by what she learned on their walk.

During the next few days, as Lillian watched the nurse caring for Julia, her eager mind probed deeply. She asked about her training, about hospitals, about the patients she treated and their needs. The work described by the young nurse was different from anything Lillian Wald had ever known; certainly it sounded grim in many ways, yet it appealed to her. How satisfying it must be to have a calling, to be of service to others, Lillian thought, over and over.

When Lillian expressed her new interest to her parents, they disapproved; they felt sure it was not a suitable life for a young lady. Nursing was just beginning to be accepted as a profession in the 1880s. Certainly it was worlds away from anything Lillian had known up to that time.

The four Wald children—Julia, Lillian, Alfred, and Gus—had been the center of attention in their family and usually had their way. Max Wald was a successful dealer in optical goods, who traveled a great deal and tried to take his family with him whenever possible, to broaden their education. Minnie Wald was a giving, trusting person, who could not do enough for her children or for anyone else who crossed her path and needed help.

Both sets of grandparents had immigrated to the United States from Central Europe. Like many other idealistic people, Jews and Christians alike, they came to the United States after the uprisings of 1848 in the German states ended in failure, and the states fell back into the hands of petty despots. Both families were Jewish, but unlike many immigrant Jews whom Lillian would befriend in later years, they had not been hounded out of Europe for their religious beliefs. They had left seeking individual freedom and opportunity; the new country had provided them with both.

The Wald family first settled in Cincinnati, where Lillian was born in 1867; later they moved to Rochester, New York, where Max Wald's business was centered. The children all attended private schools; when they were very young their grandfather would hold them spellbound for hours with tales out of the Jewish and the German traditions and readings from the world's great books. Lillian soon learned to read herself and loved to study; by the time she was sixteen she had advanced far enough in her schooling to be eligible to enter Vassar College as a sophomore. The president of the college thought she was too young and advised that she wait at least a year. Lillian went back to "Miss Cruttenden's English-French Boarding and Day School for Young Ladies and Little Girls"; by year's end, the thought of college had lost its appeal.

She read a lot, took tea with her mother's friends, went to elegant parties in the evening. There were many young men eager to dance with her, and it was all very pleasant. Yet somehow, the life of a stylish young lady left Lillian vaguely dissatisfied. For a while she did part-time work for a business firm, but that was not the answer. Five years went by. Then suddenly, during her sister's illness, she knew exactly what she wanted to do.

In later years, Lillian would look back on her childhood and conclude that she had been a spoiled child. Yet spoiled children are usually self-centered, and Lillian learned from earliest childhood to give of herself, to share, to consider the world's problems as her own. When chance opened up a door upon a world unknown to her, she saw not just the sadness and the need, but a challenge to which she must respond. She overcame her family's misgivings and entered the nursing school at New York Hospital, in New York City, in August 1889. She was then twenty-two.

She did not find it easy to adjust to the discipline of nursing school nor to the sight of suffering in others. At first she dreaded going into the operating room and put it off just as long as she could. One morning, a woman she had cared for was due for an operation; she was frightened and very apprehensive.

"I think she would feel reassured if you went with her," suggested the supervisor of nursing. Lillian wheeled her patient into the operating room. Once there, she found her help was needed, and there was little time to think or to be squeamish. And so she did what needed doing, as she would during all her years of service.

She didn't mind the long hours, the crowded living quarters, the meals, skimpy and dull, the cleaning and scrubbing she had never had to do at home. It was all worth it when a patient smiled as she walked in the ward, when she saw people responding to her care and her warm personality. What she hated were all the rules and regulations, and with those she was frequently at odds.

A few days after she had entered the hospital, she heard screams coming from a locked room, and she went in. She found herself in a padded cell, where an old man with a wild look in his eyes was yelling himself hoarse. He told Lillian he had had nothing to eat and was starving.

"Why, that's terrible!" replied the sympathetic girl. "I'll get you something."

It was Sunday, in the late afternoon, and the hospital's kitchen was locked and unsupervised. Lillian borrowed the key from a friendly elevator man, raided the refrigerator, and fed the hungry man. Monday morning she burst into the office of the nursing director and told her what she thought of the way the hospital treated its patients. Irene Sutliffe, the director, was a woman of humor and compassion, who understood her students' conflicts at the start of their training. She listened to Lillian's story, then told her that the old man was an acute alcoholic recovering from delirium tremens and had been locked up for his own safety.

"I understand how you felt," she told her charge, "but after you have been here a while I believe you will agree that a certain amount of discipline is essential." She also pointed out that the refrigerator she had raided was reserved for patients on specific diets, who had been deprived by her impulsive action. "But personally, I am glad that you fed the old man," she concluded, smiling.

Frequently, during the eighteen months of training, Lillian would find herself torn between her impetuous, independent nature and the discipline required of a nurse; with Irene Sutliffe's understanding guidance, she succeeded in reconciling the two and graduated in March 1891.

For a year she worked at an orphanage, sickened and shocked as she witnessed the harshness with which children were treated. She did what she could to protect her young charges from abuse, but after a few months she knew she did not approve of institutions for children; that was not where she wanted to be of service.

She enrolled in the Women's Medical College in New York, founded to provide women with the education that most medical schools denied them in those days. She was not destined to become a physician, but in the months of going to lectures, reading text books, bending over microscopes, caring for sick people in hospitals, she learned much about diseases and pain, about the needs of human beings in trouble. While she was attending medical school she was asked to teach a class for immigrant women in home nursing. The class met in a house on Henry Street, on the Lower East Side.

At the turn of the century, New York's Lower East Side was the first port of call for millions of immigrants from Eastern and Southern Europe. Half a million people were pouring into the United States every year; the next two decades were to bring even more. Thousands settled into the crowded tenements of Lower Manhattan. Far from finding the promised land they envisioned, they fell prey to the exploitation of landlords and employers. Often an entire family lived in one sunless, airless room; often they worked there, too, stitching garments, pressing hats, rolling cigars, or making paper flowers—whatever piece work they had been able to find.

Lillian Wald had come in contact with new immigrants during her training; she knew them as patients in a hospital, but she had never visited one of their homes. She had never been to the Lower East Side.

Teaching her classes, Lillian soon found out that her pupils had a long way to go before they could hope to become nurses. She showed them the most basic elements of keeping a city dwelling clean, of helping their families be well fed and healthy. The women knew no English; she relied on a word or two of German, on a little Hebrew learned in childhood, on a warm smile, to teach them what she could.

On a damp March morning in 1893 a little girl

broke into Lillian's class, asking for help. In tears, she explained that her mother was very ill. Mother had spoken of the friendly nurse who taught the class, the child said shyly. Would the nurse come?

Years later, Lillian Wald recalled that she had been teaching her pupils how to make a bed when the child arrived. She gathered up the sheets she had brought to class, picked up her first-aid bag, and followed the little girl out of the room, holding her hand.

"The child led me over broken roadways," Miss Wald described the day many years later, "over dirty mattresses and heaps of refuse . . . between tall, reeking houses whose laden fire escapes . . . bulged with household goods of every description. The rain added to the dismal appearance of the streets and to the discomfort of the crowds which thronged them, intensifying the odors which assailed me from every side . . . The child led me on through a tenement hallway, across a court where open and unscreened closets [toilets] were . . . used by men and women, up into a rear tenement, by slimy steps whose accumulated dirt was augmented that day by the mud of the streets, and finally into the sickroom."

There, on an unclean cot, lay the child's mother, frightened by a hemorrhage that would not stop. The family stood helplessly around; seven of them shared two windowless, dark rooms with extra boarders.

Lillian went right to work. She asked the family to bring in water from the tap they used along with everyone else on the floor. She bathed the woman, made the bed with the clean sheets she had brought, reassured the shaken husband, who was crippled and with no visible source of income. She cleaned the rooms as

best she could, then taught the older children how to care for their mother until she could come back the next day. She left some medication. Hours later, when she walked out into the crowded street, she knew that her own life had been profoundly altered, that once again a chance accident had shown her the way.

She would not go back to the medical college: that seemed too academic, too removed. She could not remain in her comfortable student quarters and merely administer to the sick in a hospital setting. She had to live among the people she wanted to help, and she must let society know of their plight.

That night she lay awake in her bed, reliving in her mind the morning's scene. Gradually she developed a plan; the next morning she described it to a friend from nursing school, Mary Brewster. They would move into the Lower East Side, Lillian suggested, give their services as nurses and "contribute our sense of citizenship," she wrote later, "to what seems an alien group in a so-called democratic society."

Mary Brewster agreed to share in the adventure. Lillian then went to seek financial aid for their plan from the woman who had backed the first nursing lessons she had given. Mrs. Solomon Loeb listened to her impassioned visitor; after Lillian left, Mrs. Loeb said to

At the turn of the century, nearly half a million immigrants from Eastern and Southern Europe poured into the United States every year. Lillian Wald showed them the basic elements of keeping a city dwelling clean and helping their families be well fed and healthy.

her daughter: "I have had a wonderful experience! I have talked to a young woman who's either crazy or a great genius!"

Mrs. Loeb promised her support and rallied a few other generous friends to do the same. After much searching, Lillian and Mary Brewster found on Jefferson Street a fifth-floor walk-up apartment with a bathroom, a rare luxury in that part of town. It was a small flat, and they furnished it simply, with cast-off pieces from their families' homes and inexpensive white curtains. Still, they knew well that on the floors below entire families shared the same amount of space they had for two, and many took in boarders to help defray the rent. Their first guest was a little boy from the basement apartment, whom they invited to stay and share their dinner. After he ate, he ran down to his mother and told her that "them ladies live like the Queen of England and eat off solid gold plates!"

Tommy was the first neighbor to drop in, but very soon the word spread that two nurses had moved into the area and were available to help the sick. At all hours of the day and often late at night people would climb the four flights of stairs to seek assistance for a sick relative or neighbor. Sometimes there was no illness; people came, as one old gentleman said, "because they said here were some ladies who would listen."

The mere fact that they were native Americans was wonderful to their fellow tenants and their neighbors. They were all recent immigrants, mostly Jews driven out by the brutal policies of the Russian tsars. Many had come from rural areas. They were unfamiliar with city ways, strange to the language and the customs, desperately in need of work and livelihood. Deprived of the counsel of their own town's elders, the village priest, or rabbi, they did not know where to turn for advice. Twenty-seven Jefferson Street, the home of Lillian Wald and Mary Brewster, became a place to which more and more people found their way.

There was much work for Lillian and her "comrade," as she called Mary Brewster. There was no visiting nurse service at the time. There were nurses available to those who could pay, and a few were hired by church groups for their members. But the concept of a nurse who would visit the home of any family regardless of church affiliation, available whether the patient could pay or not, was waiting for Lillian Wald to bring it into existence. Most sick people remained at home untreated, afraid of entering a city hospital.

There were children with measles playing in the streets; there were adults with typhoid sharing quarters with dozens of people; frequently women died in childbirth because they had been attended by unskilled midwives; every summer hundreds of babies died because the milk sold in the shops was impure. Each illness was made worse by overcrowding in the tenements, by the dirt that compounded infection, by poverty that kept people half starved and prevented them from calling doctors when needed. Public hospitals were avoided at all cost; they had a reputation for grim treatment and fearful death rates.

Right from the start, Lillian Wald realized that she couldn't stop with merely taking care of the sick. In every case, she tried to find out what had caused the illness, tried to improve conditions she found in the home. She would explain the importance of cleanliness if the patient was to get well; she would sweep the sickroom, dispose of garbage, come back again and again to make sure her instructions were being followed. She convinced people with contagious diseases to enter a hospital; she would accompany them, then visit them to help them overcome their fears. She found convalescent homes for those recently ill, arranged excursions in the country for groups of needy children. Most of all, she taught mothers how to keep their families healthy. She became social worker and teacher as well as nurse.

Two nurses could only help a handful of people every day, but Lillian Wald and Mary Brewster hoped to show by each individual success what could be done if society chose to care for its less fortunate members.

At the end of the day the two young nurses would come back to their walk-up on Jefferson Street, and late at night Lillian would write detailed reports for those whose moral and financial support enabled her to continue her work. She would note moneys spent for carfare, prescriptions, milk or eggs for a starving family, an advance on rent to save an old man from eviction. If people were destitute, the two nurses would care for them without fee. If they could pay, even only ten cents, it was accepted. Most of their patients were proud, unaccustomed to taking charity; any payment, no matter how small, helped to preserve their dignity.

"I sat in the kitchen of our little apartment with my feet in the oven," Lillian wrote many years later, remembering those early days, "as it was too cold to hold a pen in the frigid temperature of the room."

Times were hard in that depression year of 1893. Few jobs were available, wages kept falling. Then as ever, the first people laid off were those most recently arrived. Among the nurses' immigrant neighbors there was widespread need; the calls for help increased in frequency.

Day by day, Lillian and Mary Brewster made new friends. Patients whom they had treated spread word of their skill and understanding and remained ever willing to help them. Doctors, who at first had feared their competition, started calling on them for assistance. Men and women from other parts of the city and the country, anxious to improve the human condition—social reformers, writers, public servants—climbed the stairs at 27 Jefferson Street to hear about their activities and to exchange ideas.

Soon two more nurses joined them in the work, and by 1895 the project that Lillian Wald had set in motion had outgrown the small apartment. She began to look around for larger quarters. Generous men and women who had backed her efforts from the start were glad to finance the purchase of a house to be used for what soon became known as the Nurses' Settlement. She found a house for sale on Henry Street, next door to the building where she had taught her first classes in home nursing. It was a three-story, red brick house built in the 1820s with a small yard in the rear. From it came forth, during the years that followed, an astonishing flow of new ideas and measures that made their mark on the social fabric of the nation.

At 265 Henry Street, Lillian Wald was joined by a handful of dedicated nurses; her beloved comrade, Mary Brewster, could not go with them. The long hours of work, the loss of sleep, had broken Mary's frail health, and she was not able to continue in her chosen profession.

There was so much to do, those first years on Henry Street, that there was hardly time for taking stock. As the nursing staff grew from the original two to fifteen by the year 1900, it became constantly more aware of the needs that beset the neighboring community; as the group met these needs, a settlement house slowly started to develop.

Previously, there had been no place where neighborhood people could meet and talk, no place whatever where children could play except the dangerous and crowded street. One of the first things Lillian Wald did in the new house was to turn the little back yard into a playground. With the neighbors' help, the nurses planted flowers, put a pile of sand under an awning, built some swings, and asked a retired seaman to make some hammocks for the babies; this small oasis was pure joy to children and adults who spent their lives without seeing a tree. Soon they cleared two adjoining back yards; their pioneer effort became known as the "Bunker Hill" of playgrounds. It was always in use: as a kindergarten in the morning, afternoons and evenings for older children and adults. On a mild day, people would often wait in line on the sidewalk for a chance to go in.

As neighbors took to dropping in at 265 Henry Street, it became evident that certain hours had to be set aside for groups of similar interests and age, or else the nurses' entire day would be spent counseling. A club for boys was one of the first ones formed, and it grew to be one of the most rewarding activities to the members themselves and to their friend Miss Lillian. Gradually other clubs were formed, and classes organized to teach English for the newly arrived and cooking, housekeeping, and home nursing for women unaccustomed to life in New York City. Festivals were celebrated for all the nationality groups in the area. From her first day on Henry Street, Lillian Wald had been struck by the rich cultural background of her neighbors. She believed that it should be preserved, not pushed aside in favor of what she liked to call "shallow Americanism," and that the different groups had much to learn from one another.

The name "Nurses' Settlement" was changed after a while; when the boys' club team, the "American Heroes," began competing in athletic events, opposing teams would taunt them with cries of "Nurses! Nurses!" which always came out sounding like "Noices! Noices!" The name "Henry Street Settlement" gradually came into use and after a few years was made official.

Those who lived and worked at 265 Henry Street thought of it as their home and of themselves as a family. They would breakfast together every day, at seven-thirty; requests for aid would be distributed by the head worker, Lillian Wald; the morning mail and the newspaper headlines would be read and discussed for any light they might shed on problems they all encountered; then each nurse would go off on her rounds. The day was spent in caring for the sick and following through the needs of patients and their families. In the late afternoon, back at the house, each nurse would share any special knowledge or interest she might have with neighborhood people: perhaps music, folk dancing, or sewing. In time, new members were added to the staff to pursue these special interests, but for the first few years this was part of the nurses' work day, too.

At the same time Lillian Wald belonged to a Social Reform Club, which met on Tuesday nights. People came there from every field of endeavor: lawyers, doctors, journalists, philosophers, nurses, government officials, social workers—that term was just coming into use. They would discuss conditions that they saw around them and read works that might shed light on these problems. Through these gatherings Miss Wald became acquainted with a world of ideas of which she had been only half aware; there she learned about settlement houses that were being founded in other American cities. She found great stimulation in discussing theories and problems, yet her main inspiration always came in response to day-to-day experience. "Something touched my forehead," she would say at dinnertime, relating some event that had shown the need for certain action.

On visiting a home with a sick mother one day in 1900, she found a twelve-year-old boy who had been excluded from school for several years because of sores on his head. She saw that the condition would respond to simple medication; no one at school had instructed the boy in what to do. Lillian Wald asked herself how many children were needlessly deprived of education for such reasons; when she checked with her nurses, each one reported similar cases. She went to the New York City Department of Health and suggested the appointment of a nurse to each school's staff. At first nothing was done; two years later, in 1902, an epidemic of an eye disease known as trachoma emptied out many classrooms in the city. She volunteered the services of one of her staff, to show that a nurse could diagnose and treat a child right in the school. After one month authorities were convinced, and New York City provided funds for school nurses, the first of their kind in the world.

On another occasion, she noticed a serious-looking boy who would come to the settlement house with books and paper and do his homework in some quiet corner. He told her he could not study in his crowded tenement room. There was only one table at home: during the day his mother used it for the sewing that earned their meager living, at night his sister washed the dishes on it, then she ironed on it. From then on, study rooms were always set aside at 265 Henry Street, with a tutor available to help with homework or suggest books to read. Study halls in the public schools of the city, and then the nation, later followed, on Miss Wald's suggestion.

When Nurse Wald went on house calls, she was often distressed by the plight of boys and girls unable to keep up with classroom work because of physical or mental disability. She heard of a young teacher, Elizabeth Farrell, who was attempting to help handicapped children in a school nearby. Lillian Wald sought her out and invited her to join the settlement staff. Together they arranged for the first ungraded classroom for boys and girls who were handicapped or had learning disabilities.

Everything relating to children was of immense concern to Lillian Wald. Nothing saddened her more than to see them working in sweatshops and in factories. She knew that there were mine workers of eleven or twelve, little cranberry pickers in New England bogs, southern mill children, young boys tending fires in glass factories; it was true all over the United States and to her it was nothing short of criminal. There were many who shared her indignation: committees had been formed on local and state levels to promote the protection of youth. Lillian Wald and her co-worker Florence Kelley felt that such efforts could only be successful on a national level. In 1905 they conceived the idea for a federal Children's Bureau, which would gather, classify, and make public information about the status of children throughout the country. Together the two women launched a campaign to create such an agency. They mobilized hundreds of influential men and women, went as far as the White House in an attempt to gain the support of President Theodore Roosevelt. He thought it was an excellent idea—typically, his reaction was "Bully!" —and yet it took over seven years before Congress passed a bill authorizing the agency. There were strong interests at work, opposing any measure that would interfere with an employer's right to treat his workers any way he saw fit, regardless of their young age.

In 1912, when the act was signed creating a federal Children's Bureau, there was talk that Miss Wald would be appointed director. But Lillian Wald was devoted to Henry Street; her life's work was there. She was a friend to the poor and unemployed in her neighborhood, and also to the fighters for social justice, the idealists and poets arguing over glasses of tea.

She enjoyed the Yiddish theater, the Italian puppet shows, the color and variety of her part of town. She loved the people of the Lower East Side, admired their spirit, their ambition, their love of learning. Many times she reached out to the nation's capital or to state authorities in an effort to resolve specific problems, but her commitment was to Henry Street.

Ten years after Lillian Wald's arrival in Jefferson Street, her settlement house was well established and held a firm place in the affections of its neighbors. A Chinese man who had been helped by Lillian Wald called her "Heavenly Lady Number One." Any stranger in trouble would be told by the policeman on the beat, "There's a lady over on Henry Street who might help you." And help she did, following each person's problem to its source and, whenever possible, working to correct the condition. Beneath her sympathy and gentleness lay a fierce determination and the knack for knowing where to apply pressure.

"The poor and needy have found in her a friend and counselor, and the rich have been ready to respond to her call. New York needs such women," commented a supporter in 1903, on the tenth anniversary of the Henry Street Settlement. In fact, her influence spread much further than New York. By word of mouth, by articles in journals, by the appreciation of doctors and hospitals who had known her work, her reputation had spread around the world. People came from all over to learn about the settlement's work; at times it seemed as if the highways of the world crossed at 265 Henry Street. Some came on their own, some were invited, if their counsel was sought or their support toward some new crusade Miss Wald wanted to launch. She had learned that opinions could be changed and hearts won over at the "family" dinner table. Once, when she was especially concerned about the treatment of immigrant workers in the factories and labor camps of New York State, she invited the governor to dinner. The result of the dinner meeting was her appointment to a committee to study the problem and, in time, the establishment of a state Bureau of Industries and Immigration, to protect alien laborers from exploitation.

As the settlement grew, the nature of her own work began to change. She still thought of herself as a nurse, but her concept of the word broadened to include, it sometimes seemed, all of society's problems. Poor working conditions, child labor, unemployment—these were to her not abstract ills to be dealt with; they were little children carrying huge bundles of garments to be sewn in tenement sweatshops, husbands unable to provide for their large families, young girls bending for untold hours over sewing machines. What to some analysts were figures on a chart, for Lillian Wald were neighbors and friends she had visited as a nurse. She became a fighter for every progressive social cause of her day.

She was one of the first to protest police brutality against the shirt makers when they went out on strike in 1909. The strikers were young women, many still

Lillian Wald loved the people of the Lower East Side, where she founded the first Visiting Nurse Service and the Henry Street Settlement House.

in their teens, who held, Lillian Wald wrote, "a vision of a better society, where opportunities for real life will be made possible." Their grievances were given tragic impact when a fire broke out in 1911 at the Triangle Shirtwaist factory. One hundred and forty-three workers lost their lives in less than twenty minutes. Escape doors had been locked, so it was said, to prevent the theft of materials! In the wake of this tragedy, legislation to protect women workers went forward in a rush, and Lillian Wald, inspecting factories as a member of a state control board, could take some comfort in knowing that such disasters were not likely to happen again.

She was thrilled by the ideals of trade unions, and when the movement for women's suffrage gathered momentum she joined in the great fight to achieve the right to vote.

By 1913, when the Henry Street Settlement celebrated its twentieth anniversary, it had grown beyond any dream Lillian Wald might have had when she went to the Lower East Side to live. Instead of one house there were seven branch houses, in several boroughs. The settlement ran a number of vacation houses in the country, clinics and milk stations, a school for midwives. Ninety-two nurses were involved in the work, making 200,000 visits every year. The original house at 265 Henry Street offered a range of clubs and classes that involved three thousand members. There were carpentry shops and kindergartens, dancing classes, debating and literary societies, gymnasiums, a savings bank, a flourishing theater. The boys' club, the famous American Heroes, had helped to mold hundreds of street boys into businessmen and

professionals, and some were coming back to lend their
moral and financial support to a new generation.

To celebrate the twentieth anniversary, neighbors
and friends staged a pageant recalling the history of
the area. The Manahatta Indians were portrayed; the
Quakers, in the year 1806, were shown opening the
first public school in New York on Henry Street;
then followed all the nationalities who in turn had
peopled those streets during the past century: Irish,
Germans, Italians, Jews from Russia and Poland. Finally, amid cheers, came a contingent of Henry Street
nurses in their smart blue uniforms, with white collars
and cuffs. "It surely seemed," said a spectator, "as if a
wave of love had struck the block."

Behind the scenes, a generous endowment fund was
created at that time so that the nursing service would
be placed on secure footing, enabling it to keep up
with the ever-increasing demand for its services.

So many accomplishments in twenty years and so
much still to be done. And all of it, worried Lillian
Wald, all of it threatened by the dark clouds of war
on the horizon. After the summer of 1914, when
World War I broke out in Europe, there was strong
sentiment in the United States against joining the
conflict. In New York City, 1,200 women marched
along Fifth Avenue to demonstrate their opposition to
the war, women of many nationalities and backgrounds,
some white-haired, some still young girls, others carrying babies.

Lillian Wald had helped to organize this unprecedented outpouring. "Women more than men can strip
war of its glamour and its out-of-date heroisms and
patriotisms," she had said at the outset, "and see it a

demon of destruction and hideous wrong—murder devastating home and happiness." She hated war. She thought of it as the "demon of all that it has taken years to build up," as a denial of her faith in human nature. She knew that among her foreign-born neighbors there were people from all the European lands now at war with one another; in the new setting, she saw them work together as brothers and sisters. She believed in that brotherhood, and she worked with her customary passion to keep the United States out of the conflict, even as the hostilities in Europe rolled on and as American public opinion gradually slid away from neutralism and toward the Allied side.

She became president of the American Union Against Militarism, a group that tried to influence the nation's course away from intervention. Their efforts failed; in April 1917 the United States entered the conflict on the side of Great Britain, France, and Russia.

Then Lillian Wald's training as a nurse came to the fore. She thought of war as a sickness, and she had fought hard to prevent it. Now her country was at war, the disease had spread; she would do her best to reduce the suffering.

The Henry Street Settlement became a headquarters for draft registration, and staff members served on the draft board. The nurses felt that if their young neighbors must be drafted, it was best done as humanely as possible in an atmosphere that was familiar to them. Henry Street nurses cared for the families of enlisted men; Miss Wald worked to improve conditions for army nurses. As war progressed, and many doctors were called into the service, the demand for nurses rose in unprecedented fashion.

In the fall of 1918 the world-wide epidemic of influenza hit New York City; during the first four days in October, five hundred cases were reported to the nurses on Henry Street. The city was not prepared to deal with such emergency. There were not enough doctors, nurses, hospital beds, drugs, or supplies; Lillian Wald and her hard-working companions went on two shifts, tending the sick both day and night. They organized a Nurses' Emergency Council, launched a campaign that recruited hundreds of volunteers to help care for those in need. After a month the epidemic was no longer a menace; its comparatively brief duration was a source of satisfaction to the nurses involved and to the head worker at Henry Street. Yet she was anxious about the lack of preparedness that had been shown and the evident need for more trained help.

She worried, too, about the state of mind of the nation in wartime. Once war had been declared, anyone who had ever been opposed to intervention incurred suspicion from government authorities. Americans of foreign birth, those from Germany in particular, were vilified and harassed in many parts of the country. Lillian Wald could not stand by in silence; she spoke out and worked to maintain the civil rights of her neighbors in time of war.

Even among her most generous contributors there were some who could not forgive her early opposition to the war, and withdrew their support from the settlement's work. She did her best to convince such people that she believed in healing, not in violence. Often her argument convinced. Yet she had moments of confusion, of depression.

"I know that the whole world is suffering from the

war," she wrote a friend, "but I feel it down to my very toes . . . Ever since I have been conscious of my part in life I have felt consecrated to the saving of human life . . . and the expansion of good will among people, and every expression of hatred . . . fairly paralyzes me."

She was not one to stay depressed for long; the end of the war heralded a decade of intense involvement on her part. Her idealism and organizing talent made her a good choice as United States representative to numerous international conferences called to shape social services in the postwar world. She attended a conference of Red Cross Committees in France, an International Women's Conference in Switzerland; she was appointed as adviser to the League of Nations Child Welfare Division; she was even invited, in 1924, to visit Soviet Russia to advise on problems of health and child welfare. She helped set up public-health nursing in several countries.

Prior to that, in October 1919, she had been appointed to attend a nation-wide industrial conference called by President Wilson to find some common ground between employers and workers. The postwar years had seen frequent disastrous strikes; in Washington, the delegates met in an atmosphere embittered by lack of mutual trust or understanding.

Miss Wald knew well how unequal was the voice of a worker when he spoke only for himself; she spoke eloquently in favor of collective bargaining, introduced resolutions urging the abolition of child labor and medical attention in large industrial plants. She urged that wages be fixed at a level where a working man could support his family without the need of additional income from the children.

There were enlightened employers who agreed with her viewpoint, but they turned out to be a small minority. The conference broke up without agreement on any point, heralding the beginning of two decades of industrial strife.

Lillian Wald returned home to Henry Street and tried to forget her disappointment by plunging into the settlement's work. There was a new drive to be launched to raise funds for the nurses, whose services were ever more in demand. There were neighborhood problems to attend to and the health services of the entire city: as the years passed, she seemed to view all of New York City as an enlarged Henry Street family. Mayors and health commissioners took her advice to heart on such varied matters as removing garbage on a nearby street or strengthening the role of the school nurse. She used her influence to improve housing conditions on the Lower East Side, promoting efforts to have new housing built.

She grew tired sometimes. She was not one to take an elevator if she could run up the stairs nor would she remove the telephone beside her bed: she wanted to be available at all times if anyone needed help. Some of her friends tried to tell her that she was no longer a young girl, and doctors recommended that she rest once in a while, but Lillian Wald simply did not have time to grow old; there was too much to do.

On her sixtieth birthday, March 10, 1927, she came home after the day's work to find the settlement filled with friends and former club members; outside, the neighbors, joined by a delegation from police and fire stations near by, presented her with an entire box filled with pennies they had collected: $122.02 for the Visiting Nurse Service.

In later years, honors came to her often. She was awarded degrees by various colleges in recognition of her founding of the public-health nursing profession. The city presented her with the Certificate of Distinguished Service. Yet it was not certificates or degrees that most pleased her, it was the friendships she had made over the years, with people rich and poor, famous or not.

Poets and prime ministers visited Henry Street; England's socialist leader Ramsay MacDonald was a friend and supporter since his days as a young public servant; Mrs. Franklin D. Roosevelt was a frequent caller and close friend. Often a successful businessman or lawyer would write a letter or call to offer his support. It would turn out that he had been one of her "boys," well aware that he might never have achieved an education or a career without the inspiring influence of the settlement and of Miss Lillian.

Such visits, and the flow of letters from old friends, became increasingly important as ill health plagued Lillian Wald during the last decade of her life. She never regained full health after a serious operation in 1932. She spent much of her time at her country home in Westport, Connecticut, where from a shady porch or from her garden she maintained a steady correspondence with friends and organizations seeking her advice. She wrote *Windows on Henry Street*, a book about the second twenty years of the Settlement, bringing *The House on Henry Street* up to date. She read newspapers and magazines and grieved about the rise of dictatorships across the sea. Even when sickness forced her to her bed, she remained vitally concerned with the national and international scene. She had supported Franklin D. Roosevelt's candidacy in 1932 and after his election applauded the brave measures he took to bring the country out of the Depression. After years of service, she could see many of the reforms she had urged, seemingly in vain, enacted into law by the New Deal.

Some time before she died, in September 1940, a visitor had sought to understand how, in one lifetime, she had accomplished so much.

"I really love people," Lillian Wald replied.

Index